Henry Ken...

B·E·L·L-B·I·R·D·S

A·N·D · O·T·H·E·R · V·E·R·S·E·S

Henry Kendall

B·E·L·L-B·I·R·D·S

A N D · O T H E R · V E R S E S

ANGUS
& ROBERTSON
PUBLISHERS

ANGUS & ROBERTSON PUBLISHERS

Unit 4, Eden Park, 31 Waterloo Road,
North Ryde, NSW, Australia 2113, and
16 Golden Square, London W1R 4BN,
United Kingdom

First published in Australia
by Angus & Robertson Publishers in 1957
as Selected Poems of Henry Kendall
Reprinted 1975
This edition 1988

National Library of Australia
Cataloguing-in-publication data.

Kendall, Henry, 1839-1882.
  Bellbirds and other verses.

  ISBN 0 207 15906 8.

  I. Moore, T. Inglis (Tom Inglis), 1901-1978. II. Title.
  III. Title: Selected poems of Henry Kendall.

A821'.1

Printed in Australia
by Australian Print Group

ACKNOWLEDGMENTS

THE Editor wishes to express his thanks and appreciation to all those who gave valuable assistance in his researches on the life and work of Kendall and in the preparation of this volume: the officials of the Mitchell Library, Sydney, and the National Library, Canberra, for friendly and efficient services; the late Mr Frederick C. Kendall, the son of the poet, and other members of the Kendall family, for biographical data; Mr Justice J. A. Ferguson and Mr J. K. Moir, for use of Kendall MSS in their collections; the late Mr W. E. Fitz Henry, Mr Walter Stone, Mr L. F. Fitzhardinge, and Mrs R. N. Wardle, for references; Professor A. D. Hope and Miss Joan Allen, of the English Department, Canberra University College, for critical and secretarial assistance.

I am particularly indebted to the Very Rev'd Dr T. T. Reed, Dean of Adelaide, the leading authority on Kendall, for his unfailing and generous co-operation in many matters, including the use of his manuscript biography of Kendall and definitive collection of Kendall poems, together with aid in the restoration of the Kendall texts.

INTRODUCTION

WHEN Henry Kendall died in 1882 at the early age of forty-three he had achieved his life's purpose: he was accepted, both at home and in England, as the finest poet Australia had produced. In 1888 Oscar Wilde had picked him out, along with Gordon, for praise. He was the only Australian poet to win a place in such standard English anthologies as Palgrave's *The Golden Treasury* and the *Oxford Book of English Verse*. His work also influenced the South African poet Roy Campbell.* In Australia itself the judgment given by G. B. Barton in 1899, that Kendall's poetry was "the finest development of poetic genius known to Australian Literature", persisted well into the twentieth century, since in 1933 Archibald T. Strong acclaimed Kendall as one "whom many consider to be still the foremost among Australian poets".

This reputation represented a triumph for Kendall's talent and tenacity over heavy odds, since he was unfortunate in weaknesses of constitution and character, in family circumstances, and in the literary conditions of his age. Never robust, he was finally afflicted by the consumption from which his father, twin brother, and a sister also died. Shy and hypersensitive, gentle and impractical, he was handicapped by temperament in the struggle for a living; for a brief period of some six years he sought escape in drink. His kindly father was a failure, and his mother became a dipsomaniac; he was forced into crippling debt by his sisters' extravagances and his brother's dishonesty; for five years he was estranged and separated from his wife. Born and bred in poverty, for most of his life he struggled loyally to support first his mother and three sisters, and then his wife and children. Destitute for some years, he suffered starvation and a mental breakdown. Towards the end of his life he wrote, "I have led a hard life full of sorrow and toil; hence the work I have done in the domain of literature is only a poor adumbration of what I might have accomplished in happier circumstances." His singing robes, he said elsewhere, were worn only in stolen moments.

The literary conditions of his age, moreover, were unpropitious for poetry, even if he enjoyed the stimulus of small circles of writers and scholars in Sydney and Melbourne which had been denied to Charles

---

* "The subject of British Colonial poetry is a poor one. Kendall is the only good example one can take . . . Kendall had brains, he was a minor Poe . . . he has influenced me very much indeed". (Roy Campbell, in his *Broken Record*.)

Harpur, as well as wider opportunities of publication. Where Harpur had found only an embittering neglect in the 1850s, Kendall by 1881 had achieved public recognition and a following large enough to make his last volume of poems both a financial and a literary success. This only came, however, at the end of his life after much adversity. Indeed, it was part of Kendall's tragedy that he was born twenty years too early. He died just when the *Bulletin* was beginning to create a new climate of literary encouragement for the nationalist writers who flourished for the next three decades. As a self-conscious "singer of the Dawn", furthermore, he was forced to struggle in pioneering the Australian environment as a suitable theme for poetry in the 1860s and 1870s, whereas by the nineties it was accepted naturally.

Kendall was born with his twin brother Basil in a slab hut on Kirmington farm, near Milton in the Ulladulla district of the South Coast of New South Wales, on 18th April 1839. Although he was baptised Thomas Henry Kendall and for a brief period only at the time of his marriage assumed the title of Henry Clarence, he always signed his poetry and letters simply as Henry Kendall. This form, therefore, by which he wished to be known, should stand as the correct name.

His enterprising, erratic grandfather, Thomas Kendall, of Lincoln-shire farming stock, was a pioneer missionary in New Zealand under Samuel Marsden, magistrate, trader, and linguist there, a chaplain in Chile, and finally from 1827 to 1852 a timber-trader on a substantial grant of land near Ulladulla. His father, Basil Kendall, was born in England in 1807, spent his boyhood in New Zealand, went with his father to Chile and served as a lieutenant in the Chilean Navy from 1825 to 1827. Following his father to Sydney, he lived there for ten years as clerk, shopkeeper, and general commission agent. Failing in business, he settled as a farmer at Kirmington, a part of his father's grant owned by his elder brother. In Sydney in 1835 he had married Matilda (or Melinda) McNally, the daughter of an Irish policeman and ex-soldier who farmed a grant at Fairy Meadows, near Wollongong, on the South Coast.

Basil Kendall struggled vainly as a farmer, both he and his wife be-came addicted to drink, and they were living in miserable poverty when the twins, Henry and Basil, were born. About five years later he abandoned farming, worked as a clerk in Sydney, then as a shep-herd on the Clarence River on the North Coast. He kept a school at Grafton for some years before his death from consumption in 1852, when Kendall was about thirteen years old. Mild and gentlemanly, he was an affectionate father who taught his son Greek myths and legends. Kendall described him as "an accomplished scholar; but an indifferent man of business".

Kendall's mother, too, was well educated and talented; later she supported her children by teaching. It was from this vivacious irresponsible Irish mother, he thought, that he derived his poetic gifts. She encouraged his literary ambitions, and introduced him to Homer at the age of nine. He also read his Bunyan, so that as a sensitive, dreaming boy in the wilds of the North Coast he saw every bush he came across "as either an Achilles or a giant".

On the father's death the Kendalls moved to Sydney and were helped by relatives, the mother going with the twin boys to her father's farm near Wollongong. Here she taught at a small school which her boys attended. Patrick McNally, a hard taskmaster, thrashed his grandson for not looking after his sheep efficiently. "From my eleventh to my fifteenth year," wrote Kendall afterwards, "I had been following sheep: illiterate and friendless, indeed." He was equally unhappy from rough treatment when in 1855 he went to sea for a two years' voyage as a sixteen-year-old cabin boy on the whaler *Plumstead*, owned and captained by his uncle Joseph Kendall. On his return he made a home for his mother, brother, and three sisters in Sydney. After employment with his uncle Laurence Kendall (a miller), and a confectioner at Newtown, he worked as an errand boy for Biddell Brothers, sweet manufacturers at Brickfield Hill, and as assistant at a small draper's shop in Pitt Street.

From his teens Kendall wrote verses, and at nineteen had his first poem published, in 1859. He contributed verses regularly to the *Empire* from 1859 to 1862, when his friend J. Sheridan Moore, a cultured writer and editor, sponsored the publication of his *Poems and Songs*, by "the boy-poet of Australia". This appeared in October 1862, a month after the London *Athenaeum* had printed both a letter of Kendall's and two of some verses he had sent to it. Although this first volume was favourably received, it was a financial failure.

Meanwhile Kendall was fortunate in receiving encouragement from such leading literary figures in Sydney as W. B. Dalley, Daniel Deniehy, N. D. Stenhouse, and Richard Rowe. Dr John Woolley, principal of the University of Sydney, taught him Latin and French, offered him a free course at the University—which Kendall had to decline because of his family responsibilities—and gave him access to the University Library. In the widening of his education Kendall was also deeply indebted to James Lionel Michael, a lawyer, minor poet, scholar, and connoisseur of the arts. When he set up practice in Grafton, Kendall followed him in 1862 and worked as a clerk in his office. Kendall's first eager admiration for his mentor, however, gradually gave way to a more critical assessment as he himself matured.

A similar change occurred in his attitude to Charles Harpur, the second strong influence on his literary development. In 1862 he began a regular correspondence with the veteran poet, twenty-six years his senior, then struggling on his farm at Eurobodalla on the South Coast. They corresponded until Harpur's death in 1868, although they only met about six months before this. Commencing as a fervent disciple, Kendall came to exchange critical comments on equal terms. With characteristic generosity he acted as Harpur's literary agent in Sydney and did all he could to secure recognition of Harpur's poetry. Harpur, according to his widow, "had a high opinion of him, but never thought him a great poet".

In 1863 Kendall left Grafton and, after brief employment at Dungog, secured a minor post as clerk in the Survey Offices in Sydney, on thirty-five shillings a week, later raised to £150 a year. He made a home for his mother and sisters at Newtown, then at St Peters. Although his mother earned a little by teaching, he found it a struggle to make ends meet and so turned to topical journalism in his spare time. In 1865 the London *Athenaeum* published two more of his poems. In 1866 he described his life as one of "poverty, debt, ambition, and (worse than all) super-sensitiveness" in an appeal to Henry Parkes, then Colonial Secretary, who found him a clerkship at £200 a year.

On 7th June 1868 Kendall married Charlotte Rutter, whose father had been a Government Medical Officer. She was an attractive girl of eighteen with golden hair and blue eyes, ten years younger than Kendall. Earlier he had been in love with Rose Bennett, daughter of the owner of the *Empire* and the subject of his poem "Rose Lorraine". They were said to have been engaged, but parted after a quarrel. Now Kendall's hopes of happiness upon his marriage were dashed by a succession of troubles. He was deeply distressed by the death of Michael from drowning, with suspicion of suicide, and then by the death of the hapless Harpur. He became the victim of his family. His sisters virtually dispossessed him of his home and furniture, and forced him into debt, which was worsened when he had to honour a cheque for £45 forged in his name by his brother Basil. As a civil servant he could not take refuge in bankruptcy. Finally, his mother developed dipsomania and embarrassed him by coming drunk to his office. Finding his position in Sydney intolerable, therefore, he resigned his clerkship in April 1869, and went with his wife and infant daughter to Melbourne to make a living by his pen. He had been encouraged to do this by winning a prize offered by the *Australian Annual* with "A Death in the Bush".

The Melbourne venture proved disastrous. Although his second volume, *Leaves from Australian Forests*, was published in 1869 and reviewed well, it failed to sell. He tried vainly to get regular employment in the civil service or a newspaper staff position. At this stage he showed no flair for practical journalism, and his one talent of writing fine lyrics was, as a fellow writer put it, "no very marketable commodity". Although he found congenial friends in fellow members of the Yorick Club, such as George Gordon McCrae, Marcus Clarke, J. J. Shillinglaw, and especially Adam Lindsay Gordon, his despondency made it impossible for him to enter into their gaiety. He and Gordon admired each other's work, and he was deeply affected by Gordon's suicide. On the day before this he had shown Gordon the enthusiastic review of *Bush Ballads and Galloping Rhymes* he had written for the *Australasian*, but there is no truth in the legend that the two poets spent Gordon's last evening together and entered into a death pact. Kendall's own situation, however, was so desperate that he could not even afford a cab fare to go to Gordon's funeral.* Poverty and despair drove him to drinking, which aggravated his plight. He was broken-hearted when his infant daughter Araluen sickened and died when only thirteen months old; blaming himself, he suffered remorse as well as grief.

Towards the end of 1870, therefore, Mrs Kendall returned to Sydney, where her second child, Frederick Clarence, was born. Kendall followed in January 1871, and again struggled desperately to support his family by journalism. His health failing, he fell into melancholia and intemperance. His wife left him to go to her mother, and he wandered the streets of Sydney completely destitute —as Lawson and Brennan were to do years later. He had a mental breakdown and was placed by friends in Gladesville Asylum. He recovered his sanity but, broken in spirit, resumed his wanderings. Henry Parkes tells how Kendall, weak and starving, tottered to his house in Liverpool Road, after spending a night lying out in the bush. Kendall himself stated afterwards, "My mind was unhinged nearly all the time", and he referred to this period as "the Shadow of 1872".

In 1873 he sailed to Grafton to edit a local paper, but left the boat at Newcastle and started to walk to Sydney. At Gosford, weak and ill, he was rescued by the Fagans, farmers and timber merchants,

---

* In *My Father and My Father's Friends* Hugh McCrae gives the poignant letter written by Kendall on this occasion.

who took him into their home at Brisbane Water and treated him as one of their large and happy family. In return he helped the Fagan brothers on the farm and in keeping their books. He recovered his health and strength, and also, after a struggle, conquered his drinking habit. In many ways he became a new man: healthy, active, cheerful, and delighting in jokes with the Fagans. He gave up writing altogether; nothing, he wrote, would tempt him to write for money again, whilst the fate of Gordon, Michael, and Harpur proved that any attempt to win a reputation by serious writing was futile.

In 1875, after an unhappy visit to Sydney, he became clerk and storekeeper for the Fagans at their new timber agency and store at Camden Haven, near Port Macquarie on the North Coast. After misunderstandings and conflicts, with some bitterness on both sides, Kendall and his wife were finally reconciled in 1876, and she went with her two sons to live in the comfortable home built for them in the settlement now called Kendall. Here Kendall enjoyed a happy family life and the peaceful beauty of the coastal forest. Although he worked long hours at the Fagans' store, he wrote satirical verse, political paragraphs, and articles for the Sydney press. He became successful in light journalism—in ironical contrast to his previous failures.

With his confidence restored, Kendall resumed serious poetry in 1879. He wrote a successful cantata for the International Exhibition in Sydney, and won the prize of one hundred guineas for an Exhibition poem offered by the *Sydney Morning Herald*. In January 1881 his third volume, *Songs from the Mountains*, was published and sold a thousand copies. Its success was due partly to the recognition won by the Exhibition cantata and prize poem, and partly to the publicity given to the book's withdrawal on first publication in December 1880, when the publisher refused to risk a libel action by continuing to include the satire "The Song of Ninian Melville".

Kendall now had five children—three sons and two daughters—and wished to provide for their future. He appealed to Henry Parkes, who secured the creation of a new post of Inspector of Forests, and to this Kendall was appointed in April 1881 at a salary of £350 a year. He moved to a new home at Cundletown, a township on the Manning River. He was well qualified for his forestry position, but it demanded very strenuous travelling by rail, coach, and horseback, with exposure to weather, which soon affected his health. In April 1882 he fell ill on a long survey trip in the Lachlan area, and in June was taken by George Fagan from Wagga Wagga to St Vincent's Hospital, Sydney, suffering from acute consumption. In

July he was moved to a house of the Fagans at Burke Street, Red-fern, where he was nursed by his wife and died on 1st August 1882. He was buried at Waverley Cemetery, Sydney, and a public appeal raised money to provide for his widow and children. Later a second public subscription provided a monument, which was erected on his grave in 1886.

In an excellent pen portrait George Gordon McCrae pictured Kendall as of middle height, spare and thin, with blue-grey eyes, prematurely aged and heavily wrinkled in face; as nervous, shy, fond of solitude, over-sensitive, sometimes quick to take offence, yet "good-natured and amiable to a fault. He could deliver a capital lecture and he shone at times positively in conversation". Another friend remarked on how when aroused he had "a soul that burned his tongue and lightened through his eyes". He was naturally grave, often melancholy, although on occasion he indulged in banter and practical jokes. Usually gentle and affectionate, he could also be roused to anger. Thus impulsive bursts of indignation betrayed him into attacking Henry Parkes in abusive satires, despite all the friend-ship and help he had received from him. Later he apologized for this ingratitude, and Parkes magnanimously forgave the attacks and continued to befriend the wayward poet. In the vicissitudes of his relations with his wife, Kendall sometimes felt bitterly towards her, whilst she in turn had much to bear from his weaknesses and difficult moods. Yet he praised her devotion warmly, and they lived happily together with their children in the final years.

Many of Kendall's poems and letters leave the impression of a pathetic figure, unequal to the burden of life, at times both pitiable and self-pitying. His plaintive preoccupation with his misfortunes indicated a lack of stamina, just as his ill-treatment by his family showed a softness of character. On the other hand, he was a different person altogether when away from the city and living happily in his beloved bush at Brisbane Water and Camden Haven. The picture of his melancholy taciturnity in Melbourne has been the accepted one, but the Fagans enjoyed having him about because he "was such good company". Joseph Fagan recorded that "he was a good swimmer. He could ride a horse well and would be up with the best of us when yarding a fractious mob of cattle and was a good judge of a horse and knew the pedigree of every horse racing at Randwick." His satires showed a lively interest in colonial politics. His son Frederick recalled him in his closing years as "a man of striking, intellectual appearance and gentle, courteous bearing. . . . At times he had a reserved manner, due to abstraction or reflection, but was often a happy, expansive and interesting companion, joining keenly in bright or intellectual conversation. He was versed in forest lore, a lover of birds and animals, a good rider and fond of swimming and boating."

Kendall's personality was thus more complex than has been generally recognized. Varying sides of it were brought out by differing circumstances. The diffidence and melancholy alternated with an expansive cheerfulness. The introspective, tearful poet with emotions easily excited could be transformed to the practical storekeeper dealing with the business trickeries of the timbergetters with a shrewd, realistic eye, the good swimmer, or the rider galloping after the cattle. Behind the self-pity there was a strength of character which enabled him to rehabilitate himself after his breakdown, overcome his drink habit, provide a home for his family, and achieve his literary ambitions. Despite his sufferings he maintained his sustaining faiths in his poetic gift, in the value of poetry, and in God as the principle of the universe, a spirit of love and truth.

"Modest about his own work; generous in regard to his contemporaries," Kendall was summed up justly by Hugh McCrae. There was no meanness or jealousy in him: much nobility. He wrote appreciatively of many fellow poets, especially of Harpur and Gordon. Like them he was no rough bush bard, but a poet who drew on a store of culture. His judgment was independent, and his criticisms of English, Irish, and American writers as well as Australian contemporaries are sound, thoughtful, and sometimes penetrating.

A survey of the critical material on Kendall's poetry reveals widely differing estimates. His reputation rose high in his own day; lacking adequate rivals for comparison, he was naturally overrated. Then his reputation fell as tastes changed and our poetry developed, till he became underrated and was even summarily cut out of our poetic reckoning. Today Kendall's reputation has begun to rise again slightly, and it should benefit in the future from a more balanced perspective of our poetic development. Thus C. Hartley Grattan, the American critic who dismissed Kendall curtly in 1929 as "a barely respectable minor poet, leaning heavily on Wordsworth and Keats", by 1942 was stating in regard to Kendall's work that "Two facets of it are of particular importance . . . first, the valiant effort to assimilate the Australian environment to poetry, and, secondly, his dream of a utopia in Australia."

The sharp decline in Kendall's reputation was due largely to considerations not purely literary, although literary ones played a part. Even in the nineteenth century there were adverse critics who criticized Kendall for "a sentimental and even lachrymose tendency", like Alexander Sutherland in 1885, or "an imitative tendency", like J. J. Malone in 1894. Later A. G. Stephens pointed out justly "the lack of intellectual content" in Kendall's poetry, whilst other limitations also came under fire. The chief criticism, however, that developed, was on the nationalist grounds. Thus P. R. Stephensen reduced Kendall to a merely transitional figure: "From Gordon, the Englishman writing about Australia in an English way; to Kendall, the Australian writing about Australia in an English way; then to Lawson and Paterson, the Australians writing about Australia in an Australian way, is the evolution of our indigenous culture." The literature created by the bush balladists in the nineties, indeed, reacted against Kendall in two ways, producing criticism of his romantic Victorian diction and his interpretation of the landscape. Because the balladists established the idea of the arid "outback" as "the real Australia", Kendall's songs of the lush coastal country became rejected as not typical of the land. Hence arose the paradox whereby the poet who had been praised especially as an interpreter of the Australian scene was denounced by the nationalists of the 1930s and 1940s as un-Australian.

Today we can distinguish clearly the nationalist, historical, and literary criteria in judging the value of Kendall as a poet. We can clarify the confusion that has arisen because he has been assessed variously as an *Australian* poet, a pioneer in the development of our poetry, and simply as a poet.

Thus the dispute as to his "Australian" character often misses the basic point that he was a man of his times, and hence used the Victorian romantic diction then current. It betrays a lack of historic sense to condemn him for such usages as *woods, forests, meadows,* and *dells,* since the country was regarded in these terms in the 1850s and 1860s, when he began writing. Dells, moreover, still remains an exact term to describe the green recesses of the eastern coast; there is no local equivalent. Furthermore, Kendall wrote of gullies and paddocks as well as dells, and employed colloquial idiom in his bush ballads. The best songs are largely written in simple standard English. In these he effected a happy integration of the Australian scene and the literary language of his day, with all its English associations. Often he failed, naturally enough, and there is an incongruity between his subject and its treatment. His achievement, however, can only be judged in the light of the special problem he had to face in pioneering the translation of the local theme into terms of English poetry.

His vision of the landscape, too, was accepted by his contemporaries as a true picture. In a letter to James Brunton Stephens he wrote: "I was born in the forests and the mountains were my sponsors. Hence, I am saturated with the peculiar spirit of Australian scenery and in painting that scenery perhaps I excel." The critics of his day agreed almost universally that he did, indeed, excel in this respect: "Whatever opinion may be formed of his poetry it cannot be denied that it is distinctly Australian poetry" (G. B. Barton, 1866); "Kendall's poetry . . . is alone national in the sense of being evolved from the country he inhabits. It is not so much he that speaks as Australia in him." (G. Oakley, 1867.) Later A. G. Stephens concluded: "There has been no writer more generically Australian than Kendall; the Spirit of the Bush hovers over his poetry." The modern nationalist claim that Kendall was not truly "Australian", therefore, is historically inaccurate. What is really meant is that he expressed the concept of the Australian landscape held in 1860 to 1880, not that held in the twentieth century.

Historically, in fact, Kendall is important as the first poet to assimilate the Australian environment and express it with any fullness: earlier poets, such as Tompson, Wentworth, and Woolls, had only given fitful glimpses. Even Harpur, despite the keenness of his eye, had painted only a few local scenes, and these objectively, without the warmth of Kendall's passionate love of the bush. Kendall enlarged, with richer details, the variety of scene and mood introduced by Harpur. Indeed, he brought a significant development to the concept of the Australian landscape. The first concept of the early settlers was of a romantically picturesque and exotic land. This merged into one of a country marked by "gloomy monotony" or "weird melancholy", to use the phrases of Wentworth and Marcus Clarke. Harpur expressed this sombreness, associated with the tragedies of pioneer settlers, in his forceful poem "The Creek of the Four Graves". Kendall expanded it in the poems grouped together here in the section entitled "Death in the Bush". His own temperament responded to its tragic and melancholy tones. A number of lyrics also describe the harshness of the dry inland plains. He added, however, three new elements to the concept of the Australian landscape. First, he celebrated his joy in the beauty of the coastal forests, mountains, and streams—a loveliness of radiant sunlight and singing waters. In the second place, he wrote of the country not as a nostalgic exile but as a patriot hymning his homeland. Finally, he introduced that sacerdotal feeling for the bush, with qualities of religious awe and adoration, coupled with a reaching out for a universal significance, which has since become a distinctive trend in Australian nature poetry. "I recognise in Poetry," he once wrote, "a revelation of Divinity beyond all revelations: a religion past all religions." In "To a Mountain" he identifies this poetic revelation of divinity with nature, in kinship with Wordsworth and Emerson. Thus Kendall created a new Australia of the mind—a country made beautiful, beloved, and sacred.

In the historical development of Australian poetry Kendall was significant, not only for this original and seminal contribution to the assimilation of the environment, but also as the best craftsman of verse that had yet appeared, the first poet to win recognition overseas, and a pioneer in various themes and forms. He was one of the first, along with Harpur, to treat the aboriginal as a serious subject, to celebrate the explorers, and to handle historical incidents. He wrote narratives as well as lyrics. He pioneered songs of bush life—of cattle-hunters, possum-hunters, and wild kangaroos—anticipating Gordon, and was a forerunner of the bush balladists in his colloquial ballads of bullock-drivers and shingle-splitters.

Kendall's true claim to consideration, however, rests on his achievement as a genuine poet. This has been blurred by the two forms in which he has been generally represented: the few poems published in anthologies of Australian poetry fail to indicate his scope and variety, whilst the collected editions of his poems, such as those edited by Sutherland and Stevens contain so many poor verses that they swamp the finer lyrics. Kendall's ear and taste were both defective, so that he can only be judged fairly by means of a selection confined to his best work. Hence the most satisfactory Kendall to date is the selection chosen by his son, Frederick C. Kendall, despite its limitations. Here the selection has been broadened slightly to give the range of his work as well as its best quality. Thus it includes the better of the bush ballads and the satires. Two lyrics, "Rose Lorraine" and the elegy on his infant daughter, "Araluen", have also been included because of their biographical interest and popular reputation, not for their literary merits, whilst "The Far Future" has a personal and historical interest as an expression of Kendall's national outlook in the colonial period.

Since there have been many variations of readings, apparently unwarranted, by different editors, the original text has been restored as published by Kendall himself in his volumes and in periodicals. The aim has been to remove the numerous corruptions in the collections of Sutherland, Frederick Kendall, and Stevens, and provide a definitive text. In the special case of "The Glen of Arrawatta" there are actually four texts, each with variations: the undated booklet published along with the poem "Cui Bono?" under the title of *The Glen of the White Man's Grave*; the version in *Leaves from Australian Forests*, 1869; a revised and expanded version published, illustrated with engravings, by the Art-Union of Victoria in 1881 under the title of *Orara*; and a holograph manuscript of the new passages, in the National Library. The text of the *Orara* version has been adopted as the latest, but the title used in *Leaves from Australian Forests* has been preserved since it is the best known and it avoids confusion of the poem with the notable lyric "Orara". The sources of the texts are given in an index.

This selection of eighty poems has been chosen out of some three hundred poems contained in Kendall's three main volumes and other booklets, the collected edition edited by Bertram Stevens, additional poems collected by Dr T. T. Reed, uncollected poems published in various publications such as the *Bulletin* and the *Freeman's Journal*, and the manuscripts in the Mitchell Library, the National Library, and private collections. Most of the uncollected poems are of inferior quality, but the selection contains some poems not published in book form before.

In order to define and sharpen the picture of Kendall's poetic achievement, the poems have been arranged, not in the usual chronological order, but in sections which bring together poems of the various genres which Kendall cultivated. Thus the volume opens with the nature lyrics in which Kendall excels, passes on to personal lyrics and elegies, and then to the bush narratives. These sections are predominantly romantic in tone. The bush narratives form a link with the narratives and descriptive pieces on classical and biblical themes, which represent the classical or objective side of Kendall. The following sections of bush ballads and satires present him in realistic vein, whilst the final section brings together a miscellany loosely united by themes of the past and the future. It is hoped that this novel arrangement will create a fresh unity by linking associated types of poems and yet illustrate the distinctive variety of Kendall's work. It aims at giving the best of his poetry and its scope in terms of poetic values acceptable today, and thus, perhaps, presenting a new Kendall who demands revaluation as a poet.

In particular, this *Selected Poems* may bring out the fact, not commonly recognized at present, that there were three Kendalls: the romantic, the classical, and the realist poet. The traditional legend of Kendall as purely a melancholy romantic, all gentleness and pathos with no robustness or humour, gives only half the truth. True, he was largely a poet of this character. He believed that "the Poetry of Retrospection" was the best poetry: "There is at all times a mellowed beauty associated with the sunsets of yesterday which we do not find in the noon of to-day, and cannot anticipate for the morn of to-morrow." This was perhaps a rationalization of the melancholy lying in his temperament or evoked by his sufferings, since he constantly recurs to regret for the past or the wistfulness of frustration. Here he is in contrast to Mary Gilmore, another poet strongly retrospective, who looks to the past for a sturdy tradition that will build the future. Not only are Kendall's personal lyrics plaintive, but his tales of the bush past and his aboriginal verses are invariably sombre. He was an incorrigible addict to elegies. In his elegaic melancholy he is entirely romantic, just as he is in many of his nature lyrics, with their constant personal note.

From his romantic sadness Kendall extracts a grave sweetness, a melodic charm. His true talent, however, is not that of the romantic lyrist expressing his own emotions, like Burns and Shelley. Although his feeling is sincere, he lacks the poetic power to communicate it fully. Perhaps he himself gave the key to this defect when, writing of the poetic temperament, he said, "I have enough of that acute sensibility to work myself into a constant flutter of excitement." His sensibilities lay too close to the surface, and fluttered too easily, so that his emotional expression often became facile and superficial. It is a major failing that he rarely achieves a true intensity of passion— a failing of which he himself was conscious. His poems of the affections are often sentimental, often trite, and even insipid. His lapses of taste led frequently to bathos. His anger emerges in abuse, overviolent; his self-pity grows lachrymose. Grasping at tragedy, he could reach only half-way to pathos. Only a few of the poems of personal sentiment attain an even standard, such as the "The Voice in the Wild Oak", "After Many Years", "Names Upon a Stone", and "Outre Mer". Here the warm, sincere feelings are expressed simply and effectively.

Contrary to tradition, the truth about Kendall is that he wrote better when using a classical objectivity than when he is singing most subjectively as a romantic poet. In his poems on classical themes or those on biblical subjects in a neo-classical mode he can achieve the classic virtues: simplicity, clarity, detachment, and the force of economy. Thus "The Voyage of Telegonus" and "King Saul at Gilboa", like such tales of the bush as "The Glen of Arrawatta" and "A Death in the Bush", have true narrative, descriptive, and dramatic power. In such poems Kendall is stronger because he has passed beyond the enervating pathos of his personal tragedy to an impersonal vigour. It is significant that one of the worst of his elegies is "Araluen", the lament for his baby daughter, when his feelings were most deeply stirred, whilst his best elegy is the one on a nameless aboriginal in "The Last of His Tribe". "Beyond Kerguelen" shows strikingly the strength Kendall could achieve when, forgetting himself in objective description, he allowed his imagination free play.

Undoubtedly the best poems are those, such as "Orara", "Mooni", and "Araluen" (the river), where his religious passion for beauty in nature inspired him with rapture, exalted his imagination, and heightened his poetic power to describe the natural scene. In such lyrics the pattern is repeated of the poet rising to fine description, then declining into the diminuendo of the wistful, plaintive ego. His poetic salvation came when he lost his self in a wider outside world, either of nature or literature, since Kendall the poet was a far stronger character than Kendall the man.

This truth is further borne out by the realistic satires, topical verses, bush songs, and ballads. Once again Kendall exercises a native strength and liveliness when diverted from himself and his woes. The satires, although frequently heavy-handed to crudeness, carry some lusty punches. The descriptions of cattle-hunters and shingle-splitters, taken from life, are vivid and vigorous. Ballads such as "Bill the Bullock-Driver", "Jim the Splitter", and "Billy Vickers" were pioneering efforts. Naturally they did not compass the colloquial assurance of Paterson's balladry. Yet they have a similar realistic treatment, gift for characterization, and touch of ironic humour. Despite a few "literary" lapses and touches of priggishness, on the whole they come freshly, smacking of the soil. It was unfortunate that Kendall and his critics tended, in the fashion of the day, to dismiss his bush realism as not conforming to the romantic tradition of poetry then current, just as the nationalists discounted the classical pieces as un-Australian. Yet the robustness of both classical and realistic verses suggests that if Kendall had not met an early death he might well have turned from his introspective melancholy to develop this promising vein of extrovert sturdiness.

Kendall's originality has been doubted, and he has been denounced for an "unpardonable" imitative tendency. Here his imitations must be distinguished from his borrowings. Some poems are frankly imitative of the style of English writers (e.g., he published "Ogyges" with the note: "After the manner of Tennyson's 'Tithonus' and Horne's 'Orion'"), but in this he followed a long-established poetic practice, and the result must be judged on its own poetic merits. Thus "The Voyage of Telegonus" is Tennysonian, whilst "To a Mountain" is Wordsworthian; yet both are good poems. In the first the imagination shown is Kendall's own, whilst the feeling of the second is highly personal, felt on the pulse of experience. "Campaspe" has merits as an exercise "after the manner" of Swinburne.

His borrowings from the poets in whom he was saturated, on the other hand, are unconscious, except where he takes lines from Gordon with an open avowal. So, too, he freely admits that his work contains "Stray echoes from the elder notes of song", not as purposive filchings but as unwitting "plunder of perfumes". Such echoes can be detected in lines or phrases caught from Horne, Wordsworth, Patmore, and Christina Rossetti, for example. Elsewhere we find language, rhythms, and rhymes reminiscent of Poe, Longfellow, Keats, Shelley, Tennyson, and Swinburne.

Here it must be noted that, despite the influence of Swinburne in some later poems, in historical fact Kendall was Swinburnian before he had ever read Swinburne—indeed, before Swinburne had published anything but an early drama. Kendall's *Poems and Songs* appeared in 1862, whereas Swinburne's *Atalanta in Calydon* did not appear till 1865, the *Poems and Ballads* till 1866. The use of alliteration, long lines and anapestic rhythms which we regard as Swinburnian had already been employed by Kendall in his first book, in which we find the characteristic elements he developed later as his own distinctive style. As H. M. Green pointed out, "he has a marked poetic personality and a music that is quite individual, in spite of the echoes". If Kendall—like many another poet—unconsciously made minor levies, he was no mere imitator. He forged his own idiom. His emotion is always his own. His local scenes were experienced.

On the other hand, his style, if his own, like Touchstone's Audrey, was also at times, like her, "a poor thing". His language was apt but conventional, wanting that freshness and element of surprise that delight one in Neilson and McCrae. Often he succumbed to the obvious alliteration and the showy, but shallow, phrase, as when he writes:

> And, softer than slumber, and sweeter than singing,
> The notes of the bell-birds are running and ringing.

Actually the notes of the bell-bird come, not "softer than slumber", but as sharp, metallic tinkles; they also come *staccato*, not *sostenuto*: ringing, but not running. Kendall had a fatal facility with words, so that he often grew garrulous and diffuse. The original energy is dissipated in a welter of words. An equal fluency with rhythms betrayed him into metrical regularity, creating monotony. Too often his verse flows on like a stream, without variation of cadence or subtlety in the melody. His blank verse, although mellifluous or dignified, usually has not the pith and sinew of Harpur's. He never mastered the sonnet form. In the types of verse, moreover, his talent was limited. His racing rhymes miss the easiness of Gordon or Paterson. His lighter verses often show a heavy hand or fall into doggerel. His satires, with some exceptions, tend to much railing with little wit. In content his poetry as a whole has little body of ideas. The intellectual element is either conventional or tenuous, although he had the ideas of the poetic imagination.

By absolute standards these defects reduce Kendall to a minor poet. In Australian poetry his place at present would probably be somewhere near the bottom rung of the best dozen poets, along with Victor Daley. True, he is superior to both Harpur and Gordon, and to such later lyrists as Quinn and Wilmot. His work is slight, however, beside that of such philosophical and intellectual poets as Brennan and O'Dowd, Baylebridge and FitzGerald. Technically he is limited compared with such craftsmen as Slessor and Douglas Stewart. In the pure lyric, where comparison is fittest, his poetry is surpassed by the artistry of McCrae, the sudden magic of Neilson, the compressed power of Mary Gilmore at her best, and the disciplined intensity of Judith Wright.

On the other hand, Kendall is a true poet who should hold an honourable place in our poetry, a born singer, a graphic painter of landscape, and a versatile craftsman.

He still remains one of the sweetest of our singers, with a natural rhythmic flow and a melody always graceful, often memorable. In spite of the weaknesses already mentioned, he had considerable metrical skill, writing effectively in many forms. Thus he can pass from the stirring, swinging dactyls of "Beyond Kerguelen" to the grave quietness of the blank verse in "Ogyges", from the crisp ring of the couplets in "King Saul at Gilboa" to the mourning cadences of "The Last of His Tribe". Skilful craftsmanship achieves the contrast between the dignified movement of the rhetoric in "The Sydney International Exhibition", the rollicking run of "The Song of Ninian Melville", the epigrammatic curtness of "Billy Vickers", stinging like the flick of a stock-whip, and the graceful ripple of "September in Australia" or "Bell-Birds". He is usually most effective in his lyrics of short lines, where the garrulity unloosed in longer measures is curbed to an economy that still compasses a melodious grace, as in "Orara" and "Araluen". Yet "Beyond Kerguelen", as Oscar Wilde declared, "has a marvellous music about it".

As a descriptive poet he caught, like Roberts, Streeton, and Gruner in painting, the light and shade of the Australian scene. It was significant that he began his first volume with a symbolical image of sunlight: "A lyre-bird lit on a shimmering space". His work abounds in phrasing of pictorial force, as in the pictures of Kerguelen as "this leper of lands in the cold"; of the Araluen River as:

> *Daughter of grey hills of wet,*
> *Born by mossed and yellow wells—*

of "Summer's large, luxurious eyes"; of Leichhardt perishing

> *On the tracts of thirst and furnace—on the dumb, blind*
> *burning plain,*
> *Where the red earth gapes for moisture, and the wan*
> *leaves hiss for rain.*

There are memorable pictures of the bush-fire's legacy:

> *Black ghosts of trees, and sapless trunks that stood*
> *Harsh hollow channels of the fiery noise*
> *Which ran from bole to bole a year before,*
> *And grew with ruin,*

or the sunlight after rain by the Orara:

> *The air is full of mellow sounds;*
> *The wet hill-heads are bright;*
> *And, down the fall of fragrant grounds,*
> *The deep ways flame with light.*

In the finest lyrics Kendall rises to a felicity where the imaginative vision matches the music of the song.

T. INGLIS MOORE.

Canberra, 1956

CONTENTS

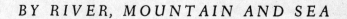

BY RIVER, MOUNTAIN AND SEA

ORARA

The strong sob of the chafing stream,
   That seaward fights its way
Down crags of glitter, dells of gleam,
   Is in the hills today.

But, far and faint, a grey-winged form
   Hangs where the wild lights wane:
The phantom of a bygone storm—
   A ghost of wind and rain.

The soft white feet of Afternoon
   Are on the shining meads:
The breeze is as a pleasant tune
   Amongst the happy reeds.

The fierce, disastrous flying fire,
   That made the great caves ring,
And scarred the slope and broke the spire,
   Is a forgotten thing.

The air is full of mellow sounds;
   The wet hill-heads are bright;
And, down the fall of fragrant grounds,
   The deep ways flame with light.

A rose-red space of stream I see
   Past banks of tender fern:
A radiant brook, unknown to me
   Beyond its upper turn.

The singing silver life I hear,
   Whose home is in the green
Far-folded woods of fountains clear
   Where I have never been.

Ah, brook above the upper bend,
   I often long to stand
Where you in soft cool shades descend
   From the untrodden Land!

Ah, folded woods that hide the grace
    Of moss and torrents strong,
I often wish to know the face
    Of that which sings your song!

But I may linger, long, and look
    Till night is over all:
My eyes will never see the brook,
    Or sweet strange waterfall!

The world is round me with its heat,
    And toil, and cares that tire:
I cannot with my feeble feet
    Climb after my desire.

But, on the lap of lands unseen,
    Within a secret zone,
There shine diviner gold and green
    Than man has ever known.

And where the silver waters sing,
    Down hushed and holy dells,
The flower of a celestial Spring—
    A tenfold splendour, dwells.

Yea, in my dream of fall and brook
    By far sweet forests furled,
I see that light for which I look
    In vain through all the world.

The glory of a larger sky
    On slopes of hills sublime
That speak with God and Morning, high
    Above the ways of Time!

Ah! haply, in this sphere of change
    Where shadows spoil the beam
It would not do to climb that range
    And test my radiant Dream.

The slightest glimpse of yonder place,
    Untrodden and alone,
Might wholly kill that nameless grace
    The charm of the Unknown.

And therefore, though I look and long,
    Perhaps the lot is bright
Which keeps the river of the song
    A beauty out of sight.

BELL-BIRDS

By channels of coolness the echoes are calling,
And down the dim gorges I hear the creek falling:
It lives in the mountain where moss and the sedges
Touch with their beauty the banks and the ledges.
Through breaks of the cedar and sycamore bowers
Struggles the light that is love to the flowers;
And, softer than slumber, and sweeter than singing,
The notes of the bell-birds are running and ringing.

The silver-voiced bell-birds, the darlings of daytime!
They sing in September their songs of the May-time;
When shadows wax strong, and the thunder-bolts hurtle,
They hide with their fear in the leaves of the myrtle;
When rain and the sunbeams shine mingled together,
They start up like fairies that follow fair weather;
And straightway the hues of their feathers unfolden
Are the green and the purple, the blue and the golden.

October, the maiden of bright yellow tresses,
Loiters for love in these cool wildernesses;
Loiters, knee-deep, in the grasses, to listen,
Where dripping rocks gleam and the leafy pools glisten:
Then is the time when the water-moons splendid
Break with their gold, and are scattered or blended
Over the creeks, till the woodlands have warning
Of songs of the bell-bird and wings of the Morning.

Welcome as waters unkissed by the summers
Are the voices of bell-birds to thirsty far-comers.
When fiery December sets foot in the forest,
And the need of the wayfarer presses the sorest,
Pent in the ridges for ever and ever
The bell-birds direct him to spring and to river,
With ring and with ripple, like runnels whose torrents
Are toned by the pebbles and leaves in the currents.

Often I sit, looking back to a childhood,
Mixt with the sights and the sounds of the wildwood,
Longing for power and the sweetness to fashion,
Lyrics with beats like the heart-beats of Passion;—
Songs interwoven of lights and of laughters
Borrowed from bell-birds in far forest-rafters;
So I might keep in the city and alleys
The beauty and strength of the deep mountain valleys:
Charming to slumber the pain of my losses
With glimpses of creeks and a vision of mosses.

BEYOND KERGUELEN*

Down in the South, by the waste without sail on it—
    Far from the zone of the blossom and tree—
Lieth, with winter and whirlwind and wail on it,
    Ghost of a land by the ghost of a sea.
Weird is the mist from the summit to base of it;
    Sun of its heaven is wizened and grey;
Phantom of light is the light on the face of it—
    Never is night on it, never is day!
Here is the shore without flower or bird on it—
    Here is no litany sweet of the springs:
Only the haughty, harsh thunder is heard on it—
    Only the storm with a roar in its wings!

Shadow of moon is the moon in the sky of it—
    Wan as the face of a wizard, and far!
Never there shines from the firmament high of it
    Grace of the planet or glory of star.
All the year round, in the place of white days on it—
    All the year round, where there never is night—
Lies a great sinister, bitter, blind haze on it:
    Growth that is neither of darkness nor light!
Wild is the cry of the sea in the caves by it—
    Sea that is smitten by spears of the snow.
Desolate songs are the songs of the waves by it—
    Down in the South where the ships never go.

Storm from the Pole is the singer that sings to it
    Hymns of the land at the planet's grey verge.
Thunder discloses dark wonderful things to it—
    Thunder, and rain, and the dolorous surge.
Hills, with no hope of a wing or a leaf on them,

---

* Oscar Wilde wrote of this lyric: " . . . the poem entitled *Beyond Kerguelen* has a marvellous music about it, a wonderful rhythm of words and a real richness of utterance. Some of the lines are strangely powerful, and, indeed, in spite of its exaggerated alliteration, or perhaps in consequence of it, the whole poem is a most remarkable work of art."

Discussing Kendall, Roy Campbell wrote: ". . . his *Kerguelen* is the father of my Tristan da Cunha. He seized first of all in verse that mystery of the lonely island walking on the sea."

Scarred with the chronicles written by flame,
Stare, through the gloom of inscrutable grief on them,
    Down on the horns of the gulfs without name.
Cliffs, with the records of fierce flying fires on them—
    Loom over perilous pits of eclipse:
Alps, with anathema stamped in the spires on them—
    Out by the wave with a curse on its lips.

Never is sign of soft beautiful green on it—
    Never the colour, the glory of rose!
Neither the fountain nor river is seen on it:
    Naked its crags are, and barren its snows!
Blue as the face of the drowned is the shore of it—
    Shore, with the capes of indefinite cave.
Strange is the voice of its wind, and the roar of it
    Startles the mountain and hushes the wave.
Out to the south, and away to the north of it,
    Spectral and sad are the spaces untold!
All the year round a great cry goeth forth of it—
    Sob of this leper of lands in the cold.

No man hath stood all its bleak bitter years on it—
    Fall of a foot on its wastes is unknown:
Only the sound of the hurricane's spears on it,
    Breaks, with the shout from the uttermost zone.
Blind are its bays with the shadow of bale on them;
    Storms of the nadir their rocks have uphurled;
Earthquake hath registered deeply its tale on them—
    Tale of distress from the dawn of the world!
There are the gaps with the surges that seethe in them—
    Gaps in whose jaws is a menace that glares!
There, the wan reefs with the merciless teeth in them
    Gleam on a chaos that startles and scares!

Back in the dawn of this beautiful sphere, on it—
    Land of the dolorous, desolate face—
Beamed the blue day; and the bountiful year on it
    Fostered the leaf and the blossom of grace,
Grand were the lights of its midsummer noon on it—
    Mornings of majesty shone on its seas:
Glitter of star and the glory of moon on it
    Fell, in the march of the musical breeze.

Valleys and hills, with the whisper of wing in them,
  Dells of the daffodil—spaces impearled,
Flowered and flashed with the splendour of Spring in them—
  Back in the morn of this wonderful world.

Soft were the words that the thunder then said to it—
  Said to this lustre of emerald plain:
Sun brought the yellow, the green, and the red to it—
  Sweet were the songs of its silvery rain.
Voices of water and wind in the bays of it
  Lingered, and lulled like the psalm of a dream.
Fair were the nights, and effulgent the days, of it—
  Moon was in shadow and shade in the beam.
Summer's chief throne was the marvellous coast of it,
  Home of the Spring was its luminous lea!
Garden of glitter! but only the ghost of it
  Moans in the South by the ghost of a sea.

ARALUEN

River, myrtle-rimmed, and set
    Deep amongst unfooted dells—
Daughter of grey hills of wet,
    Born by mossed and yellow wells—

Now that soft September lays
    Tender hands on thee and thine,
Let me think of blue-eyed days,
    Star-like flowers, and leaves of shine!

Cities soil the life with rust:
    Water-banks are cool and sweet:
River, tired of noise and dust
    Here I come to rest my feet.

Now the month from shade to sun
    Fleets and sings supremest songs,
Now the wilful woodwinds run
    Through the tangled cedar throngs.

Here are cushioned tufts and turns
    Where the sumptuous noontide lies.
Here are seen by flags and ferns
    Summer's large luxurious eyes.

On this spot wan Winter casts
    Eyes of ruth, and spares its green
From his bitter sea-nursed blasts,
    Spears of rain and hailstones keen.

Rather here abideth Spring,
    Lady of a lovely land,
Dear to leaf and fluttering wing,
    Deep in blooms—by breezes fanned.

Faithful friend beyond the main—
    Friend that Time nor Change makes cold—
Now, like ghosts, return again
    Pallid perished days of old.

Ah, the days—the old, old theme
　　Never stale, but never new,
Floating, like a pleasant dream,
　　Back to me and back to you.

Since we rested on these slopes,
　　Seasons fierce have beaten down
Ardent loves and blossoming hopes—
　　Loves that lift, and hopes that crown.

But, believe me, still mine eyes
　　Often fill with light that springs
From divinity, which lies
　　Ever at the heart of things.

Solace do I sometimes find
　　Where you used to hear with me
Songs of stream and forest-wind,
　　Tones of wave and harp-like tree.

Araluen! home of dreams!
　　Fairer for its flowerful glade
Than the face of Persian streams,
　　Or the slopes of Syrian shade.

Why should I still love it so?
　　Friend and brother far away,
Ask the winds that come and go,
　　What hath brought me here today.

Evermore of you I think,
　　When the leaves begin to fall,
Where our river breaks its brink,
　　And a rest is over all.

Evermore in quiet lands,
　　Friend of mine beyond the sea,
Memory comes with cunning hands,
　　Stays, and paints your face for me.

SEPTEMBER IN AUSTRALIA

Grey Winter hath gone, like a wearisome guest,
    And, behold, for repayment,
September comes in with the wind of the West,
    And the Spring in her raiment!
The ways of the frost have been filled of the flowers
    While the forest discovers
Wild wings with the halo of hyaline hours,
    And a music of lovers.

September, the maid with the swift, silver feet!
    She glides, and she graces
The valleys of coolness, the slopes of the heat,
    With her blossomy traces.
Sweet month with a mouth that is made of a rose,
    She lightens and lingers
In spots where the harp of the evening glows,
    Attuned by her fingers.

The stream from its home in the hollow hill slips
    In a darling old fashion;
And the day goeth down with a song on its lips,
    Whose key-note is passion.
Far out in the fierce bitter front of the sea,
    I stand and remember
Dead things that were brothers and sisters of thee,
    Resplendent September.

The West, when it blows at the fall of the noon,
    And beats on the beaches,
Is filled with a tender and tremulous tune
    That touches and teaches:
The stories of Youth, of the burden of Time,
    And the death of Devotion,
Come back with the wind, and are themes of the rhyme,
    In the waves of the ocean.

We, having a secret to others unknown,
    In the cool mountain-mosses,
May whisper together, September, alone
    Of our loves and our losses.

One word for her beauty, and one for the grace
    She gave to the hours;
And then we may kiss her, and suffer her face
    To sleep with the flowers.

High places that knew of the gold and the white
    On the forehead of Morning,
Now darken and quake, and the steps of the Night
    Are heavy with warning!
Her voice in the distance is lofty and loud,
    Through the echoing gorges;
She hath hidden her eyes in a mantle of cloud,
    And her feet in the surges!

On the tops of the hills; on the turreted cones—
    Chief temples of thunder—
The gale, like a ghost, in the middle watch moans,
    Gliding over and under.
The sea, flying white through the rack and the rain,
    Leapeth wild at the forelands;
And the plover, whose cry is like passion with pain,
    Complains in the moorlands.

O, season of changes—of shadow and shine—
    September the splendid!
My song hath no music to mingle with thine,
    And its burden is ended:
But thou, being born of the winds and the sun,
    By mountain, by river,
May lighten and listen, and loiter and run,
    With thy voices for ever.

MOONI

(Written in the Shadow of 1872)

Ah, to be by Mooni now!
Where the great dark hills of wonder,
Scarred with storm and cleft asunder
By the strong sword of the thunder,
   Make a night on morning's brow!
Just to stand where Nature's face is
Flushed with power in forest places—
Where of God authentic trace is—
   Ah, to be by Mooni now!

Just to be by Mooni's springs!
There to stand, the shining sharer
Of that larger life, and rarer
Beauty caught from beauty fairer
   Than the human face of things!—
Soul of mine from sin abhorrent
Fain would hide by flashing current,
Like a sister of the torrent,
   Far away by Mooni's springs.

He that is by Mooni now,
Sees the water-sapphires gleaming
Where the River Spirit dreaming
Sleeps by fall and fountain streaming
   Under lute of leaf and bough!—
Hears, where stamp of Storm with stress is,
Psalms from unseen wildernesses
Deep amongst far hill-recesses—
   He that is by Mooni now.

Yea, for him by Mooni's marge,
Sings the yellow-haired September
With the face the gods remember
When the ridge is burnt to ember,
   And the dumb sea chains the barge!

Where the mount like molten brass is,
Down beneath fern-feathered passes
Noonday dew in cool green grasses
   Gleams on him by Mooni's marge.

   Who that dwells by Mooni yet,
Feels, in flowerful forest arches,
Smiting wings and breath that parches
Where strong Summer's path of march is,
   And the suns in thunder set?
Housed beneath the gracious kirtle
Of the shadowy water-myrtle—
Winds may hiss with heat and hurtle
   He is safe by Mooni yet!

   Days there were when he who sings
(Dumb so long through Passion's losses)
Stood where Mooni's water crosses
Shining tracts of green-haired mosses,
   Like a soul with radiant wings:
Then the psalm the wind rehearses—
Then the song the stream disperses,
Lent a beauty to his verses—
   Who tonight of Mooni sings.

   Ah, the theme—the sad grey theme!
Certain days are not above me,
Certain hearts have ceased to love me,
Certain fancies fail to move me
   Like the affluent morning dream.
Head whereon the white is stealing,
Heart whose hurts are past all healing,
Where is now the first pure feeling?—
   Ah, the theme—the sad grey theme!

   Sin and Shame have left their trace!
He who mocks the mighty, gracious
Love of Christ, with eyes audacious,
Hunting after fires fallacious,

Wears the issue in his face.
Soul that flouted gift and Giver,
Like the broken Persian river
Thou hast lost thy strength for ever!—
    Sin and Shame have left their trace.

In the years that used to be,
When the large supreme occasion
Brought the life of inspiration,
Like a god's transfiguration
    Was the shining change in me.
Then, where Mooni's glory glances,
Clear diviner countenances
Beamed on me like blessed chances
    In the years that used to be.

Ah, the beauty of old ways!
Then the man who so resembled
Lords of light unstained, unhumbled,
Touched the skirts of Christ, nor trembled
    At the grand benignant gaze!
Now he shrinks before the splendid
Face of Deity offended—
All the loveliness is ended:
    All the beauty of old ways!

Still to be by Mooni cool—
Where the water-blossoms glister,
And, by gleaming vale and vista,
Sits the English April's sister,
    Soft and sweet and wonderful!
Just to rest beyond the burning
Outer world—its sneers and spurning—
Ah, my heart—my heart is yearning
    Still to be by Mooni cool!

Now, by Mooni's fair hill heads,
Lo, the gold green lights are glowing
Where, because no wind is blowing,

Fancy hears the flowers growing
  In the herby watersheds!
Faint it is—the sound of thunder
From the torrents far thereunder,
Where the meeting mountains ponder—
  Now, by Mooni's fair hill heads.

  Just to be where Mooni is!
Even where the fierce fall races
Down august unfathomed places
Where of sun or moon no trace is,
  And the streams of shadow hiss!
Have I not an ample reason
So to long for—sick of treason—
Something of the grand old season?
  Just to be where Mooni is?

THE AUSTRAL MONTHS

MARCH

Clear upland voices full of wind and stream
Greet March, the sister of the flying beam
And speedy shadow. She with rainbow crowned
Lives in a sphere of songs of many sound.
The hymn of waters, and the gale's high tone,
With anthems from the thunder's mountain throne,
Are with her ever. This, behold, is she
Who draws its great cry from the strong sad sea!
She is the month of majesty. Her force
Is power that moves along a stately course
Within the lines of order, like no wild
And lawless strength of winter's fiercest child.
About her are the wind-whipped torrents. Far
Above her gleams and flies the stormy star:
And round her, through the highlands and their rocks,
Rings loud the grand speech from the equinox.

APRIL

The darling of Australia's autumn. Lo,
Down dewy dells the strong, swift torrents flow!
This is the month of singing waters. Here
A tender radiance fills the southern year,
No bitter winter sets on herb and root
Within the gracious glades, a frosty foot;
The spears of sleet—the arrows of the hail,
Are here unknown. But down the dark green dale
Of moss and myrtle, and the herby streams
This April wanders in a home of dreams.
Her flower-soft name makes language falter. All
Her paths are soft and cool; and runnels fall
In music round her; and the woodlands sing
For evermore with voice of wind and wing,
Because this is the month of beauty—*this*
The crowning grace of all the grace that is.

High travelling winds, filled with the strong Storm's soul,
Are here with dark strange sayings from the Pole.
Now is the time when every great cave rings
With sharp clear echoes caught from mountain springs—
This is the season when all torrents run
Beneath no bright, glad beauty of the sun—
Here, where the trace of last year's green is lost,
Are haughty gales and lordship of the frost!
Far down, by fields forlorn and forelands bleak,
Are wings that fly not—birds that never speak.
But, in the deep hearts of the glens unseen,
Stand grave mute forests of eternal green;
And here the lady born in wind and rain
Comes oft to moan and clap her palms with pain.
This is our wild-faced July, in whose breast
Is never faultless light or perfect rest.

ILLA CREEK

A strong sea-wind flies up and sings
  Across the blown-wet border,
Whose stormy echo runs and rings
  Like bells in wild disorder.

Fierce breath hath vext the foreland's face,
  It glistens, glooms, and glistens;
But deep within this quiet place
  Sweet Illa lies and listens.

Sweet Illa of the shining sands,
  She sleeps in shady hollows
Where August flits with flowerful hands
  And silver Summer follows.

Far up the naked hills is heard
  A noise of many waters;
But green-haired Illa lies unstirred
  Amongst her star-like daughters.

The tempest pent in moaning ways
  Awakes the shepherd yonder;
But Illa dreams, unknown to days
  Whose wings are wind and thunder.

Here fairy hands and floral feet
  Are brought by bright October;
Here stained with grapes, and smit with heat,
  Comes Autumn sweet and sober.

Here lovers rest, what time the red
  And yellow colours mingle,
And Daylight droops with dying head
  Beyond the western dingle.

And here, from month to month, the time
  Is kissed by Peace and Pleasure,
While Nature sings her woodland rhyme
  And hoards her woodland treasure.

Ah, Illa Creek! ere Evening spreads
    Her wings o'er towns unshaded,
How oft we seek thy mossy beds
    To lave our foreheads faded!

For, let me whisper, then we find
    The strength that lives, nor falters,
In wood and water, waste and wind,
    And hidden mountain altars.

TO A MOUNTAIN

To thee, O Father of the stately peaks,
Above me in the loftier light—to thee,
Imperial brother of those awful hills
Whose feet are set in splendid spheres of flame,
Whose heads are where the gods are, and whose sides
Of strength are belted round with all the zones
Of all the world, I dedicate these songs.
And, if within the compass of this book,
There lives and glows *one* verse in which there beats
The pulse of wind and torrent—if *one* line
Is here that like a running water sounds,
And seems an echo from the lands of leaf,
Be sure that line is thine. Here in this home
Away from men and books and all the schools,
I take thee for my Teacher. In thy voice
Of deathless majesty, I, kneeling, hear
God's grand authentic gospel! Year by year,
The great sublime cantata of thy storm
Strikes through my spirit—fills it with a life
Of startling beauty! Thou my Bible art
With holy leaves of rock, and flower, and tree,
And moss, and shining runnel. From each page
That helps to make thy awful Volume, I
Have learned a noble lesson. In the psalm
Of thy grave winds, and in the liturgy
Of singing waters, lo! my soul has heard
The higher worship; and from thee indeed
The broad foundations of a finer hope
Were gathered in; and thou hast lifted up
The blind horizon for a larger faith!
Moreover, walking in exalted woods
Of naked glory—in the green and gold
Of forest sunshine—I have paused like one
With all the life transfigured; and a flood
Of light ineffable has made me feel
As felt the grand old prophets caught away
By flames of inspiration; but the words
Sufficient for the story of my Dream
Are far too splendid for poor human lips!
But thou to whom I turn with reverent eyes—

O stately Father whose majestic face
Shines far above the zone of wind and cloud
Where high dominion of the morning is—
Thou hast the Song complete of which my songs
Are pallid adumbrations! Certain sounds
Of strong authentic sorrow in this book
May have the sob of upland torrents—these,
And only these, may touch the great World's heart;
For lo! they are the issues of that Grief
Which makes a man more human, and his life
More like that frank exalted life of thine.
But in these pages there are other tones
In which thy large superior voice is not—
Through which no beauty that resembles thine
Has ever shone. *These* are the broken words
Of blind occasions when the World has come
Between me and my Dream. No song is here
Of mighty compass; for my singing robes
I've worn in stolen moments. All my days
Have been the days of a laborious life;
And ever on my struggling soul has burned
The fierce heat of this hurried sphere. But thou
To whose fair majesty I dedicate
My book of rhymes—thou hast the perfect rest
Which makes the heaven of the highest gods!
To thee the noises of this violent time
Are far faint whispers; and, from age to age,
Within the world and yet apart from it
Thou standest! Round thy lordly capes the sea
Rolls on with a superb indifference
For ever: in thy deep green gracious glens
The silver fountains sing for ever. Far
Above dim ghosts of waters in the caves,
The royal robe of morning on thy head
Abides for ever! evermore the wind
Is thy august companion; and thy peers
Are cloud, and thunder, and the face sublime
Of blue midheaven! On thy awful brow
Is Deity; and in that voice of thine
There is the great imperial utterance
Of God for ever; and thy feet are set
Where evermore, through all the days and years,
There rolls the grand hymn of the deathless wave.

COOGEE

Sing the song of wave-worn Coogee—Coogee in the distance white
With its jags and points disrupted, gaps and fractures fringed with
light!
Haunt of gledes and restless plovers of the melancholy wail
Ever lending deeper pathos to the melancholy gale.
There, my brothers, down the fissures, chasms deep and wan and
wild,
Grows the sea-bloom, one that blushes like a shrinking fair blind
child;
And amongst the oozing forelands many a glad green rock-vine
runs,
Getting ease on earthy ledges sheltered from December suns.

Often, when a gusty morning, rising cold and grey and strange,
Lifts its face from watery spaces, vistas full with cloudy change;
Bearing up a gloomy burden which anon begins to wane,
Fading in the sudden shadow of a dark determined rain;
Do I seek an eastern window, so to watch the breakers beat
Round the steadfast crags of Coogee, dim with drifts of driving sleet:
Hearing hollow mournful noises sweeping down a solemn shore
While the grim sea-caves are tideless and the storm strives at their
core.

Often when the floating vapours fill the silent autumn leas,
Dreamy memories fall like moonlight over silver sleeping seas,
Youth and I and Love together!—other times and other themes
Come to me unsung, unwept for, through the faded evening gleams:
Come to me and touch me mutely—I that looked and longed so well,
Shall I look and yet forget them? who may know or who foretell?
Though the southern wind roams, shadowed with its immemorial
grief,
Where the frosty wings of Winter leave their whiteness on the leaf?

Friend of mine beyond the waters, here and here these perished days
Haunt me with their sweet dead faces and their old divided ways.
You that helped and you that loved me, take this song and when
you read
Let the lost things come about you, set your thoughts and hear and
heed:

Time has laid his burden on us: we who wear our manhood now—
We would be the boys we *have* been, free of heart and bright of
brow—
Be the boys for just an hour, with the splendour and the speech
Of thy lights and thunders, Coogee, flying up thy gleaming beach!

Heart's desire and heart's division! who would come and say to me
With the eyes of far-off friendship, "You are as you used to be"?
Something glad and good has left me here with sickening discontent,
Tired of looking, neither knowing, what it was or where it went.
So it is this sight of Coogee, shining in the morning dew,
Sets me stumbling through dim summers once on fire with youth and
you.
Summers pale as southern evenings when the year has lost its power,
And the wasted face of April weeps above the withered flower.

Not that seasons bring no solace—not that time lacks light and rest;
But the old things were the dearest, and the old loves seem the best.
We that start at songs familiar—we that tremble at a tone,
Floating down the ways of music, like a sigh of sweetness flown,
We can never feel the freshness—never find again the mood
Left amongst fair-featured places brightened of our brotherhood;
This, and this, we have to think of, when the night is over all,
And the woods begin to perish, and the rains begin to fall.

MOUNTAIN MOSS

It lies amongst the sleeping stones,
 Far down the hidden mountain-glade;
And past its brink the torrent moans
 For ever in a dreamy shade:

A little patch of dark-green moss,
 Whose softness grew of quiet ways,
(With all its deep, delicious floss,)
 In slumb'rous suns of summer days.

You know the place? With pleasant tints
 The broken sunset lights the bowers;
And then the woods are full with hints
 Of distant, dear, voluptuous flowers!

'Tis often now the pilgrim turns
 A faded face towards that seat,
And cools his brow amongst the ferns:
 The runnel dabbling at his feet.

There fierce December seldom goes,
 With scorching step, and dust, and drouth;
But, soft and low, October blows
 Sweet odours from her dewy mouth.

And Autumn, like a gipsy bold,
 Doth gather near it grapes and grain,
Ere Winter comes, the woodman old,
 To lop the leaves in wind and rain.

O, greenest moss of mountain glen,
 The face of Rose is known to thee;
But we shall never share with men
 A knowledge dear to Love and me!

For are they not between us saved,
 The words my darling used to say;
What time the western waters laved
 The forehead of the fainting Day!

Cool comfort had we on your breast
    While yet the fervid Noon burned mute
O'er barley field and barren crest,
    And leagues of gardens flushed with fruit.

Oh! sweet and low, we whispered so;
    And sucked the pulp of plum and peach:
But it was many years ago,
    When each, you know, was loved of each.

ARAKOON

Lo, in storms, the triple-headed
    Hill, whose dreaded
Bases battle with the seas,
Looms across fierce widths of fleeting
    Waters beating
Evermore on roaring leas!

Arakoon, the black, the lonely!
    Housed with only
Cloud and rain-wind, mist and damp:
Round whose foam-drenched feet, and nether
    Depths, together
Sullen sprites of thunder tramp!

There the East hums loud and surly,
    Late and early,
Through the chasms and the caves;
And across the naked verges
    Leap the surges!
White and wailing waifs of waves.

Day by day, the sea-fogs gathered—
    Tempest-fathered—
Pitch their tents on yonder peak!
Yellow drifts and fragments, lying
    Where the flying
Torrents chafe the cloven creek!

And at nightfall, when the driven
    Bolts of heaven
Smite the rock and break the bluff,
Thither troop the elves whose home is
    Where the foam is,
And the echo, and the clough.

Ever girt about with noises,
    Stormy voices,
And the salt breath of the strait,

Stands the steadfast Mountain Giant,
 Grim, reliant,
Dark as Death, and firm as Fate!

So when trouble treads, like thunder,
 Weak men under—
Treads, and breaks the thews of these—
Set thyself to bear it bravely,
 Greatly, gravely,
Like the hill in yonder seas:

Since the wrestling, and endurance
 Give assurance
To the faint at bay with pain,
That no soul to strong Endeavour
 Yoked for ever,
Works against the tide in vain.

SYDNEY HARBOUR

Where Hornby, like a mighty fallen star,
Burns through the darkness with a splendid ring
Of tenfold light; and where the awful face
Of Sydney's northern headland stares all night
On dark, determined waters from the east,
From year to year a wild, Titanic voice
Of fierce aggressive Sea shoots up, and makes,
When Storm sails high through drifts of driving sleet,
And in the days when limpid waters glass
December's sunny hair and forest face,
A roaring, down by immemorial caves—
A thunder in the everlasting hills.

But, calm and lucid as an English lake,
Beloved by beams and wooed by wind and wing,
Shut in from tempest-trampled wastes of wave,
And sheltered from white wraths of surge by walls—
Grand ramparts founded by the hand of God,
The lordly Harbour gleams! Yea, like a shield
Of marvellous gold dropt in his fiery flight
By some lost angel in the elder days,
When Satan faced and fought Omnipotence,
It shines amongst fair-flowering hills, and flows
By dells of glimmering greenness manifold;
And all day long when soft-eyed Spring comes round
With gracious gifts of bird, and leaf, and grass;
And through the noon when sumptuous Summer sleeps
By yellowing runnels under beetling cliffs,
This royal Water blossoms far and wide
With ships from all the corners of the world.
And while sweet Autumn with her gipsy face
Stands in the gardens, splashed from heel to thigh
With spinning vine-blood—yea, and when the mild,
Wan face of our Australian Winter looks
Across the congregated southern fens,
Then low, melodious, shell-like songs are heard
Beneath proud hulls and pompous clouds of sail,

By yellow beaches under lisping leaves,
In hidden nooks to Youth and Beauty dear,
And where the ear may catch the counter-voice
Of Ocean, travelling over far, blue tracts.

Moreover, when the Moon is gazing down
Upon her lovely reflex in the wave,
(What time she, sitting in the zenith, makes
A silver silence over stirless woods),
Then, where its echoes start at sudden bells,
And where its waters gleam with flying lights,
The Haven lies, in all its beauty clad,
More lovely even than the golden lakes
The poet saw, while dreaming splendid dreams
Which showed his soul the far Hesperides.

MOSS ON A WALL

Dim dreams it hath of singing ways,
    Of far-off woodland water-heads,
And shining ends of April days
    Amongst the yellow runnel beds.

Stoop closer to the ruined wall,
    Wherein the wilful wilding sleeps,
As if its home were waterfall
    By dripping clefts and shadowy steeps!

A little waif, whose beauty takes
    A touching tone, because it dwells
So far away from mountain lakes,
    And lily leaves, and lightning fells.

Deep hidden in delicious floss
    It nestles, sister, from the heat:
A gracious growth of tender moss,
    Whose nights are soft, whose days are sweet.

Swift gleams across its petals run,
    With winds that hum a pleasant tune:
Serene surprises of the sun,
    And whispers from the lips of Noon.

The evening-coloured apple-trees
    Are faint with July's frosty breath;
But lo, this stranger getteth ease
    And shines amidst the strays of Death!

And at the turning of the year,
    When August wanders in the cold,
The raiment of the nursling here
    Is rich with green and glad with gold.

O, friend of mine, to one whose eyes
    Are vext because of alien things,
For ever in the wall moss lies
    The peace of hills and hidden springs.

From faithless lips and fickle lights
   The tired pilgrim sets his face,
And thinketh here of sounds and sights
   In many a lovely forest-place.

And when by sudden fits and starts
   The sunset on the moss doth burn,
He often dreams, and lo, the marts
   And streets are changed to dells of fern!

For, let me say, the wilding placed
   By hands unseen amongst these stones,
Restores a Past by Time effaced,
   Lost loves and long-forgotten tones!

As sometimes songs and scenes of old
   Come faintly unto you and me.
When winds are wailing in the cold,
   And rains are sobbing on the sea.

EUROCLYDON

On the storm-cloven Cape
    The bitter waves roll
    With the bergs of the Pole,
And the darks and the damps of the Northern Sea:
    For the storm-cloven Cape
    Is an alien Shape
With a fearful face; and it moans, and it stands
    Outside all lands
        Everlastingly!

When the fruits of the year
    Have been gathered in Spain;
    And the Indian rain
Is rich on the evergreen lands of the Sun;
    There comes to this Cape—
    To this alien Shape,
As the waters beat in and the echoes troop forth,
    The Wind of the North,
        Euroclydon!

And the wilted thyme,
    And the patches past
    Of the nettles cast
In the drift of the rift, and the broken rime,
    Are tumbled and blown
    To every zone
With the famished glede, and the plovers thinned
    By this fourfold Wind—
        This Wind sublime!

On the wrinkled hills
    By starts and fits
    The wild Moon sits;
And the rindles fill, and flash, and fall
    In the way of the light,
    Through the straitened night,
When the sea-heralds clamour, and elves of the war
    In the torrents afar,
        Hold festival!

From ridge to ridge
The polar fires
On the naked spires
With a foreign splendour, flit and flow;
And clough and cave
And architrave,
Have a blood-coloured glamour on roof and on wall,
Like a nether hall
In the hells below!

The dead dry lips
Of the ledges, split
By the thunder fit
And the stress of the sprites of the forkéd flame,
Anon break out
With a shriek and a shout,
Like a hard bitter laughter cracked and thin
From a ghost with a sin
Too dark for a name!

And, all thro' the year,
The fierce seas run
From sun to sun
Across the face of a vacant world!
And the Wind flies forth
From the wild white North,
That shivers and harries the heart of things,
And shapes with its wings
A Chaos uphurled!

Like one who sees
A rebel light
In the thick of the night,
As he stumbles and staggers on summits afar—
Who looks to it still,
Up hill and hill,
With a steadfast hope (though the ways be deep,
And rough, and steep),
Like a steadfast star;

So I, that stand
On the outermost peaks
Of peril, with cheeks
Blue with the salts of a frosty Sea,

Have learnt to wait
With an eye elate
And a heart intent, for the fuller blaze
Of the Beauty that rays
Like a glimpse for me—

Of the Beauty that grows
Whenever I hear
The Winds of Fear
From the tops and the bases of barrenness call:
And the duplicate lore
Which I learn evermore,
Is of Harmony filling and rounding the Storm,
And the marvellous Form
That governs all!

NARRARA CREEK
(*Written in the Shadow of 1872*)

From the rainy hill-heads where, in starts and in spasms,
Leaps wild the white torrent from chasms to chasms—
From the home of bold echoes whose voices of wonder
Fly out of blind caverns struck black by high thunder—
Through gorges august in whose nether recesses
Is heard the far psalm of unseen wildernesses—
Like a dominant spirit, a strong-handed sharer
Of spoil with the tempest, comes down the Narrara.

Yea, where the great sword of the hurricane cleaveth
The forested fells that the dark never leaveth—
By fierce-featured crags in whose evil abysses
The clammy snake coils and the flat adder hisses—
Past lordly rock temples where Silence is riven
By the anthems supreme of the four winds of heaven—
It speeds with the cry of the streams of the fountains
It chained to its sides and dragged down from the mountains!

But when it goes forth from the slopes with a sally—
Being strengthened with tribute from many a valley—
It broadens, and brightens, and thereupon marches
Above the stream-sapphires and under green arches
With the rhythm of majesty—careless of cumber—
Its might in repose and its fierceness in slumber—
Till it beams on the plains where the wind is a bearer
Of words from the sea to the stately Narrara!

Narrara, grand son of the haughty hill torrent!
Too late in my day have I looked at thy current—
Too late in my life to discern and inherit
The soul of thy beauty—the joy of thy spirit!
With the years of the youth and the hairs of the hoary,
I sit like a shadow outside of thy glory;
Nor look with the morning-like feelings, O River,
That illumined the boy in the days gone for ever.

Ah! sad are the sounds of old ballads which borrow
One half of their grief from the listener's sorrow;
And sad are the eyes of the pilgrim who traces
The ruins of Time in revisited places;
But sadder than all is the sense of his losses
That cometh to one when a sudden age crosses
And cripples his manhood. So stricken by fate, I
Felt older at thirty than some do at eighty.

Because I believe in the beautiful story—
The poem of Greece in the days of her glory—
That the high-seated Lord of the woods and the waters
Has peopled His world with His deified daughters—
That flowerful forests and waterways streaming
Are gracious with goddesses glowing and gleaming—
I pray that thy singing divinity, fairer
Than wonderful women, may listen, Narrara!

O Spirit of sea-going currents—thou being
The child of immortals all-knowing, all-seeing—
Thou hast at thy heart the dark truth that I borrow
For the song that I sing thee no fanciful sorrow;
In the sight of thine eyes is the history written
Of Love smitten down as the strong leaf is smitten;
And before thee there goeth a phantom beseeching
For faculties forfeited—hopes beyond reaching!

Thou knowest, O sister of deities blazing
With splendour ineffable—beauty amazing,
What life the gods gave me—what largess I tasted
The youth thrown away and the faculties wasted!
I might, as thou seest, have stood in high places
Instead of in pits where the brand of disgrace is:
A by-word for scoffers—a butt, and a caution,
With the grave of poor Burns and Maginn for my portion.

But the heart of the Father Supreme is offended,
And my life in the light of His favour is ended;
And, whipped by inflexible devils, I shiver
With a hollow "*too late*" in my hearing for ever;
But thou, being sinless, exalted, supernal,
The daughter of diademed gods—the eternal,
Shalt shine in thy waters when Time and Existence
Have dwindled like stars in unspeakable distance!

37

But the face of thy river—the torrented power
That smites at the rock while it fosters the flower—
Shall gleam in my dreams with the summer-look splendid,
And the beauty of woodlands and waterfalls blended;
And often I'll think of far forested noises,
And the emphasis deep of grand sea-going voices;
And turn to Narrara the eyes of a lover
When the sorrowful days of my singing are over.

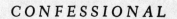

CONFESSIONAL

DEDICATION

To her, who, cast with me in trying days,
Stood in the place of health, and power, and praise;—
Who, when I thought all light was out, became
A lamp of hope that put my fears to shame;—
Who faced for love's sole sake the life austere
That waits upon the man of letters here;—
Who, unawares, her deep affection showed,
By many a touching little wifely mode;—
Whose spirit self-denying, dear, divine,
Its sorrows hid, so it might lessen mine,—
To her, my bright best friend, I dedicate
This book of songs. 'Twill help to compensate
For much neglect. The act, if not the rhyme,
Will touch her heart and lead her to the time
Of trials past. That which is most intense
Within these leaves is of her influence;
And if aught here is sweetened with a tone
Sincere, like love, it came of love alone.

PREFATORY SONNETS

I

I purposed once to take my pen and write
    Not songs like some tormented and awry
    With Passion, but a cunning harmony
Of words and music caught from glen and height,
And lucid colours born of woodland light,
    And shining places where the sea-streams lie;
But this was when the heat of youth glowed white,
    And since I've put the faded purpose by.
I have no faultless fruits to offer you
    Who read this book; but certain syllables
    Herein are borrowed from unfooted dells,
And secret hollows dear to noontide dew;
And these at least, though far between and few,
    May catch the sense like subtle forest spells.

II

So take these kindly, even though there be
    Some notes that unto other lyres belong:
    Stray echoes from the elder sons of Song;
And think how from its neighbouring, native sea
The pensive shell doth borrow melody.
    I would not do the lordly masters wrong,
    By filching fair words from the shining throng
Whose music haunts me, as the wind a tree!
    Lo, when a stranger, in soft Syrian glooms
Shot through with sunset, treads the cedar dells,
And hears the breezy ring of elfin bells
    Far down by where the white-haired cataract booms,
He, faint with sweetness caught from forest smells,
    Bears thence, unwitting, plunder of perfumes.

AFTER MANY YEARS

The song that once I dreamed about,
　　The tender, touching thing,
As radiant as the rose without—
　　The love of wind and wing—
The perfect verses to the tune
　　Of woodland music set,
As beautiful as afternoon,
　　Remain unwritten yet.

It is too late to write them now,
　　The ancient fire is cold:
No ardent lights illume the brow
　　As in the days of old.
I cannot dream the dream again;
　　But, when the happy birds
Are singing in the sunny rain,
　　I think I hear its words.

I think I hear the echo still
　　Of long forgotten tones,
When evening winds are on the hill,
　　And sunset fires the cones.
But only in the hours supreme
　　With songs of land and sea,
The lyrics of the leaf and stream,
　　This echo comes to me.

No longer doth the earth reveal
　　Her gracious green and gold:
I sit where youth was once, and feel
　　That I am growing old.
The lustre from the face of things
　　Is wearing all away:
Like one who halts with tired wings,
　　I rest and muse today.

There is a river in the range
　　I love to think about:
Perhaps the searching feet of change
　　Have never found it out.

Ah! oftentimes I used to look
    Upon its banks, and long
To steal the beauty of that brook
    And put it in a song.

I wonder if the slopes of moss
    In dreams so dear to me—
The falls of flower and flower-like floss—
    Are as they used to be!
I wonder if the waterfalls,
    The singers far and fair
That gleamed between the wet green walls,
    Are still the marvels there!

Ah! let me hope that in that place
    The old familiar things
To which I turn a wistful face,
    Have never taken wings.
Let me retain the fancy still
    That, past the lordly range,
There always shines, in folds of hill,
    One spot secure from change!

I trust that yet the tender screen
    That shades a certain nook
Remains, with all its gold and green,
    The glory of the brook!
It hides a secret, to the birds
    And waters only known—
The letters of two lovely words:
    A poem on a stone.

Perhaps the lady of the past
    Upon these lines may light:
The purest verses and the last
    That I may ever write.
She need not fear a word of blame;
    Her tale the flowers keep;
The wind that heard me breathe her name
    Has been for years asleep.

But, in the night, and when the rain
    The troubled torrent fills,
I often think I see again
    The river in the hills.
And when the day is very near,
    And birds are on the wing,
My spirit fancies it can hear
    The song I cannot sing.

THE MUSE OF AUSTRALIA

Where the pines with the eagles are nestled in rifts,
And the torrent leaps down to the surges,
I have followed her, clambering over the clifts,
By the chasms and moon-haunted verges.
I know she is fair as the angels are fair,
For have I not caught a faint glimpse of her there;
A glimpse of her face, and her glittering hair,
     And a hand with the Harp of Australia?
I never can reach you, to hear the sweet voice
So full with the music of fountains!
Oh! when will you meet with that soul of your choice,
Who will lead you down here from the mountains?—
A lyre-bird lit on a shimmering space;
It dazzled mine eyes, and I turned from the place,
And wept in the dark for a glorious face,
     And a hand with the Harp of Australia!

REST

Sometimes we feel so spent for want of rest,
    We have no thought beyond. I know today,
    When tired of bitter lips and dull delay
With faithless words, I cast mine eyes upon
The shadows of a distant mountain-crest,
And said, "That hill must hide within its breast
Some secret glen secluded from the sun.
    O, mother Nature! would that I could run
Outside to thee, and, like a wearied guest
    Half blind with lamps and sick of feasting, lay
An aching head on thee. Then down the streams
    The moon might swim; and I should feel her grace,
    While soft winds blew the sorrows from my face
So quiet in the fellowship of dreams."

ROSE LORRAINE

Sweet water-moons, blown into lights
  Of flying gold on pool and creek,
And many sounds, and many sights,
  Of younger days, are back this week.
I cannot say I sought to face,
  Or greatly cared to cross again,
The subtle spirit of the place
  Whose life is mixed with Rose Lorraine.

What though her voice rings clearly through
  A nightly dream I gladly keep,
No wish have I to start anew
  Heart-fountains that have ceased to leap.
Here, face to face with different days,
  And later things that plead for love,
It would be worse than wrong to raise
  A phantom far too fain to move.

But, Rose Lorraine—ah, Rose Lorraine,
  I'll whisper now where no one hears.
If you should chance to meet again
  The man you kissed in soft dead years,
Just say for once "he suffered much",
  And add to this "his fate was worst
Because of me, my voice, my touch",—
  There is no passion like the first!

If I that breathe your slow sweet name
  As one breathes low notes on a flute,
Have vext your peace with word of blame,
  The phrase is dead—the lips are mute.
Yet when I turn towards the wall,
  In stormy nights, in times of rain,
I often wish you could recall
  Your tender speeches, Rose Lorraine.

Because, you see, I thought them true,
    And did not count you self-deceived,
And gave myself in all to you,
    And looked on Love as Life achieved.
Then came the bitter, sudden change,
    The fastened lips, the dumb despair:
The first few weeks were very strange,
    And long, and sad, and hard to bear.

No woman lives with power to burst
    My passion's bonds, and set me free;
For Rose is last where Rose was first,
    And only Rose is fair to me.
The faintest memory of her face,
    The wilful face that hurt me so,
Is followed by a fiery trace
    That Rose Lorraine must never know.

I keep a faded ribbon string
    You used to wear about your throat;
And of this pale, this perished thing,
    I think I know the threads by rote.
God help such love! To touch your hand,
    To loiter where your feet might fall,
You marvellous girl, my soul would stand
    The worst of hell—its fires and all!

THE VOICE IN THE WILD OAK

(Written in the Shadow of 1872)

Twelve years ago, when I could face
    High heaven's dome with different eyes—
In days full flowered with hours of grace,
    And nights not sad with sighs—
I wrote a song in which I strove
    To shadow forth thy strain of woe,
Dark widowed sister of the grove—
    Twelve wasted years ago.

But youth was then too young to find
    Those high authentic syllables
Whose voice is like the wintering wind
    By sunless mountain fells;
Nor had I sinned and suffered then
    To that superlative degree
That I would rather seek than men
    Wild fellowship with thee.

But he who hears this autumn day
    Thy more than deep autumnal rhyme,
Is one whose hair was shot with grey
    By Grief instead of Time.
He has no need, like many a bard,
    To sing imaginary pain,
Because he bears, and finds it hard,
    The punishment of Cain.

No more he sees the affluence
    Which makes the heart of Nature glad;
For he has lost the fine first sense
    Of Beauty that he had.
The old delight God's happy breeze
    Was wont to give, to grief has grown;
And therefore, Niobe of trees,
    His song is like thine own.

But I who am that perished soul
　　Have wasted so these powers of mine,
That I can never write that whole
　　Pure, perfect speech of thine.
Some lord of words august, supreme,
　　The grave, grand melody demands;
The dark translation of thy theme
　　I leave to other hands.

Yet here, where plovers nightly call
　　Across dim melancholy leas—
Where comes by whistling fen and fall
　　The moan of far off seas—
A grey old Fancy often sits
　　Beneath thy shade with tired wings,
And fills thy strong, strange rhyme by fits
　　With awful utterings.

Then times there are when all the words
　　Are like the sentences of one
Shut in by fate from wind and birds
　　And light of stars and sun!
No dazzling dryad but a dark
　　Dream-haunted spirit, doomed to be
Imprisoned, crampt in bands of bark,
　　For all eternity.

Yea, like the speech of one aghast
　　At Immortality in chains,
What time the lordly storm rides past
　　With flames and arrowy rains!
Some wan Tithonus of the wood
　　White with immeasurable years—
An awful ghost in solitude
　　With moaning moors and meres!

And when high thunder smites the hill,
　　And hunts the wild dog to his den,
Thy cries, like maledictions, shrill
　　And shriek from glen to glen!
As if a frightful memory whipped
　　Thy soul for some infernal crime
That left it blasted, blind, and stript—
　　A dread to Death and Time!

But when the fair-haired August dies,
    And flowers wax strong and beautiful,
Thy songs are stately harmonies
    By wood-lights green and cool.
Most like the voice of one who shows
    Through sufferings fierce, in fine relief,
A noble patience and repose—
    A dignity in grief.

But ah! conceptions fade away,
    And still the life that lives in thee—
The soul of thy majestic lay—
    Remains a mystery!
And he must speak the speech divine—
    The language of the high-throned lords,
Who'd give that grand old theme of thine
    Its sense in faultless words.

By hollow lands and sea-tracts harsh
    With ruin of the fourfold gale,
Where sighs the sedge and sobs the marsh,
    Still wail thy lonely wail.
And, year by year, one step will break
    The sleep of far hill-folded streams;
And seek, if only for thy sake,
    Thy home of many dreams.

ARALUEN

Take this rose and very gently place it on the tender, deep
Mosses where our little darling Araluen, lies asleep.
Put the blossom close to baby—kneel with me, my love, and pray;
We must leave the bird we've buried—say good-bye to her today
In the shadow of our trouble, we must go to other lands;
And the flowers we have fostered will be left to other hands.
Other eyes will watch them growing—other feet will softly tread.
Where two hearts are nearly breaking: where so many tears are shed.
Bitter is the world we live in: life and love are mixed with pain—
We will never see these daisies: never water them again.

Ah, the saddest thought in leaving baby in this bush alone
Is that we have not been able on her grave to place a stone!
We have been too poor to do it; but, my darling, never mind!
God is in the gracious heavens, and His sun and rain are kind.
They will dress the spot with beauty, they will make the grasses
      grow:
Many winds will lull our birdie—many songs will come and go.
Here the blue-eyed Spring will linger—here the shining month will
      stay
Like a friend by Araluen, when we two are far away;
But, beyond the wild wide waters, we will tread another shore:
We will never watch this blossom—never see it any more.

Girl, whose hand at God's high altar in the dear dead year I pressed,
Lean your stricken head upon me: this is still your lover's breast!
She who sleeps was first and sweetest—none we have to take her
      place!
Empty is the little cradle, absent is the little face.
Other children may be given; but this rose beyond recall—
But this garland of your girlhood will be dearest of them all.
None will ever, Araluen, nestle where you used to be,
In my heart of hearts, you darling, when the world was new to me.
We were young when you were with us. Life and Love were happy
      things
To your father and your mother ere the angels gave you wings.

You that sit and sob beside me—you upon whose golden head
Many rains of many sorrows have from day to day been shed—
Who, because your love was noble, faced with me the lot austere
Ever pressing with its hardship on the man of letters here—
Let me feel that you are near me: lay your hand within mine own.
You are all I have to live for, now that we are left alone.
Three there were but one has vanished. Sins of mine have made you
    weep;
But forgive your baby's father now that baby is asleep.
Let us go, for night is falling—leave the darling with her flowers:
Other hands will come and tend them—other friends, in other hours.

NAMES UPON A STONE

(Inscribed to G. L. Fagan, Esq.)

Across bleak widths of broken sea
    A fierce north-easter breaks,
And makes a thunder on the lea—
    A whiteness of the lakes.
Here, while beyond the rainy stream
    The wild winds sobbing blow,
I see the river of my dream
    Four wasted years ago.

Narrara of the waterfalls,
    The darling of the hills,
Whose home is under mountain walls
    By many-luted rills!
Her bright green nooks and channels cool
    I never more may see;
But ah! the Past was beautiful—
    The sights that used to be.

There was a rock-pool in a glen
    Beyond Narrara's sands;
The mountains shut it in from men,
    In flowerful fairy lands;
But once we found its dwelling place—
    The lovely and the lone;
And, in a dream, I stooped to trace
    Our names upon a stone.

Above us. where the starlike moss
    Shone on the wet green wall
That spanned the straitened stream across,
    We saw the waterfall.
A silver singer far away
    By folded hills and hoar,
Its voice is in the woods today—
    A voice I hear no more.

I wonder if the leaves that screen
    The rock-pool of the past
Are yet as soft and cool and green
    As when we saw them last!
I wonder if that tender thing,
    The moss, has overgrown
The letters by the limpid spring—
    Our names upon the stone!

Across the face of scenes we know
    There may have come a change;
The places seen four years ago
    Perhaps would now look strange.
To you, indeed, they cannot be
    What haply once they were:
A friend beloved by you and me
    No more will greet us there.

Because I know the filial grief
    That shrinks beneath the touch—
The noble love whose words are brief,
    I will not say too much.
But often, when the night-winds strike
    Across the sighing rills,
I think of him whose life was like
    The rock-pool's in the hills.

A beauty like the light of song
    Is in my dreams that show
The grand old man who lived so long
    As spotless as the snow.
A fitting garland for the dead
    I cannot compass yet;
But many things he did and said
    I never will forget.

In dells where once we used to rove
    The slow sad water grieves;
And ever comes from glimmering grove
    The liturgy of leaves.
But time and toil have marked my face—
    My heart has older grown,
Since, in the woods, I stooped to trace
    Our names upon the stone.

TO FANNY*

To Fanny with the dear good face,
　　The brightest of our throng,
I come with purer thoughts than love
　　Can give, to help my song.

She glides through life, a gentle light,
　　A sweetness round us thrown:
A Mary in the house of God,
　　A Martha in her own.

---

* Miss Fanny Edwards.

ON A STREET*

I dread that street! Its haggard face
    I have not seen for eight long years—
A mother's curse is on the place:
    (There's blood, my reader, in her tears.)
No child of man shall ever track
    Through filthy dust the singer's feet;
A fierce old memory drags me back—
    I hate its name—I dread that street.

Upon the lap of green sweet lands,
    Whose months are like your English Mays,
I try to hide in Lethe's sands
    The bitter old Bohemian days.
But Sorrow speaks in singing leaf,
    And trouble talketh in the tide;
The skirts of a stupendous grief
    Are trailing ever at my side.

I will not say who suffered there:
    'Tis best the name aloof to keep,
Because the world is very fair—
    Its light should sing the dark to sleep.
But—let me whisper—in that street
    A woman, faint through want of bread,
Has often pawned the quilt and sheet,
    And wept upon a barren bed.

How gladly would I change my theme,
    Or cease the song and steal away,
But on the hill, and by the stream
    A ghost is with me night and day!

---

* The few who know the story of poor W——— of Melbourne will perhaps
see force in these uncoloured verses.—H.K.

Both the feelings shown and the circumstances described in this poem indi-
cate that it deals with Kendall himself, his wife, and his infant child Araluen
during his tragic plight in Melbourne. His note appears to be an attempt to
disguise this fact, like his original title of "On a Sydney Street", scored out
by him in the holograph manuscript of the poem in the National Library,
Canberra.—Ed.

A dreadful darkness, full of wild
Chaotic visions comes to me:
I seem to hear a dying child—
Its mother's face I seem to see.

Here surely on this bank of bloom
My verse with shine should overflow;
But ah, it comes—the rented room,
With man and wife who suffered so!
From flower and leaf there is no hint—
I only see a sharp distress:
A lady in a faded print,
A careworn writer for the Press.

I only hear the brutal curse
Of landlord clamouring for his pay;
And yonder is the pauper's hearse
That comes to take a child away.
Apart, and with the half-grey head
Of sudden age, again I see
The father writing by the dead
To earn the undertaker's fee.

No tear at all is asked for him—
A drunkard well deserves his life;
But voice will quiver—eyes grow dim
For her, the patient, pure young wife,
The gentle girl of better days,
As timid as a mountain fawn,
Who used to choose untrodden ways,
And place at night her rags in pawn.

She could not face the lighted square,
Or show the street her poor thin dress;
In one close chamber, bleak and bare,
She hid her burden of distress.
Her happy schoolmates used to drive
On gaudy wheels the town about:
The meal that keeps a dog alive
She often had to go without.

I tell you this is not a tale
    Conceived by me but bitter truth!
Bohemia knows it pinched and pale
    Beside the pyre of burnt-out Youth!
These eyes of mine have often seen
    The sweet girl-wife, in winters rude,
Steal out at night through courts unclean,
    To hunt about for chips of wood.

Have I no word at all for him
    Who used down fetid lanes to slink,
And squat in taproom corners grim,
    And drown his thoughts in dregs of drink?
This much I'll say, that, when the flame
    Of Reason re-assumed its force,
The hell the Christian fears to name
    Was heaven to his fierce remorse.

Just think of him—beneath the ban,
    And steeped in sorrow to the neck!
Without a friend—a feeble man
    In failing health—a human wreck!
With all his sense and scholarship,
    How could he face his fading wife?
The devil never lifted whip
    With strings like these that scourged his life!

But He, in whom the dying thief
    Upon the Cross did place his trust,
Forgets the sin and feels the grief,
    And lifts the sufferer from the dust.
And now, because I have a dream
    The man and woman found the light;
A glory burns upon the stream—
    With gold and green the woods are bright.

But—still I hate that haggard street—
    Its filthy courts, its alleys wild!
In dreams of it I always meet
    The phantom of a wailing child.
The name of it begets distress—
    Ah, Song, be silent! show no more
The lady in the perished dress—
    The scholar on the taproom floor!

FAITH IN GOD

Have faith in God. For whosoever lists
    To calm conviction in these days of strife,
Will learn that in this steadfast stand exists
    The scholarship severe of human life—

This face to face with Doubt! I know how strong
    His thews must be who fights, and falls, and bears,
By sleepless nights, and vigils lone and long,
    And many a woeful wraith of wrestling prayers;

Yet trust in Him! not in an old Man throned
    With thunders on an everlasting cloud,
But in that awful Entity, enzoned
    By no wild wraths nor bitter homage loud.

When from the summits of some sudden steep
    Of Speculation, you have strength to turn
To things too boundless for the broken sweep
    Of finite comprehension, wait and learn

That God hath been "His own interpreter"
    From first to last;—so you will understand
The tribe who best succeed when men most err
    To suck through fogs the fatness of the land.

One thing is surer than the autumn tints
    We saw last week in yonder river bend,
That all our poor expression helps and hints,
    However vaguely, to the solemn end

That God is Truth. And if our dim ideal
    Fall short of fact—so short that we must weep,
Why shape specific sorrows, though the real
    Be not the song which erewhile made us sleep?

Remember, Truth draws upward! This, to us,
    Of steady happiness should be a cause
Beyond the differential calculus,
    Or Kant's dull dogmas and mechanic laws.

A man is manliest when he wisely knows
    How vain it is to halt, and pule, and pine,
Whilst under every mystery haply flows
    The finest issue of a love divine.

OUTRE MER

I see, as one in dreaming,
    A broad, bright, quiet sea;
Beyond it lies a haven—
    The only home for me.
Some men grow strong with trouble,
    But all my strength is past,
And tired and full of sorrow,
    I long to sleep at last.
By force of chance and changes
    Man's life is hard at best;
And, seeing rest is voiceless,
    The dearest thing is rest.

Beyond the sea—behold it,
    The home I wish to seek,
The refuge of the weary,
    The solace of the weak!
Sweet angel fingers beckon,
    Sweet angel voices ask
My soul to cross the waters;
    And yet I dread the task.
God help the man whose trials
    Are tares that he must reap!
He cannot face the future—
    His only hope is sleep.

Across the main a vision
    Of sunset coasts, and skies,
And widths of waters gleaming,
    Enchant my human eyes.
I, who have sinned and suffered,
    Have sought—with tears have sought—
To rule my life with goodness,
    And shape it to my thought.
And yet there is no refuge
    To shield me from distress,
Except the realm of slumber
    And great forgetfulness.

IN MEMORIAM

CHARLES HARPUR

Where Harpur lies, the rainy streams,
    And wet hill-heads, and hollows weeping,
Are swift with wind, and white with gleams,
    And hoarse with sounds of storms unsleeping.

Fit grave it is for one whose song
    Was tuned by tones he caught from torrents,
And filled with mountain-breaths, and strong
    Wild notes of falling forest-currents.

So let him sleep! the rugged hymns
    And broken lights of woods above him!
And let me sing how Sorrow dims
    The eyes of those that used to love him.

As April in the wilted wold
    Turns faded eyes on splendours waning,
What time the latter leaves are old,
    And ruin strikes the strays remaining;

So we that knew this singer dead,
    Whose hands attuned the Harp Australian,
May set the face and bow the head,
    And mourn his fate and fortunes alien.

The burden of a perished faith
    Went sighing through his speech of sweetness,
With human hints of Time and Death,
    And subtle notes of incompleteness.

But when the fiery power of Youth
    Had passed away and left him nameless,
Serene as Light, and strong as Truth,
    He lived his life untired and tameless.

And, far and free, this man of men
    With wintry hair and wasted feature,
Had fellowship with gorge and glen,
    And learned the loves and runes of Nature.

Strange words of wind, and rhymes of rain,
　　And whispers from the inland fountains,
Are mingled in his various strain
　　With leafy breaths of piny mountains.

But, as the under-currents sigh
　　Beneath the surface of a river,
The music of Humanity
　　Dwells in his forest-psalms for ever.

No soul was he to sit on heights
　　And live with rocks apart and scornful:
Delights of men were his delights,
　　And common troubles made him mournful.

THE LATE MR A. L. GORDON

IN MEMORIAM

At rest! Hard by the margin of that sea
Whose sounds are mingled with his noble verse,
Now lies the shell that never more will house
The fine, strong spirit of my gifted friend.
Yea, he who flashed upon us suddenly,
A shining soul with syllables of fire,
Who sang the first great songs these lands can claim
To be their own; the one who did not seem
To know what royal place awaited him
Within the Temple of the Beautiful,
Has passed away; and we who knew him sit
Aghast in darkness, dumb with that great grief
Whose stature yet we cannot comprehend;
While over yonder churchyard, hearsed with pines,
The night wind sings its immemorial hymn,
And sobs above a newly-covered grave.

The bard, the scholar, and the man who lived
That frank, that open-hearted life which keeps
The splendid fire of English chivalry
From dying out; the one who never wronged
A fellowman; the faithful friend who judged
The many, anxious to be loved of him,
By what he saw, and not by what he heard,
As lesser spirits do; the brave great soul
That never told a lie, or turned aside
To fly from danger—he, as I say, was one
Of that bright company this sin-stained world
Can ill afford to lose.

                They did not know,
The hundreds who had read his sturdy verse
And revelled over ringing major notes,
The mournful meaning of the undersong
Which runs through all he wrote, and often takes
The deep autumnal, half-prophetic tone
Of forest winds in March; nor did they think

That on that healthy-hearted man there lay
The wild specific curse which seems to cling
For ever to the Poet's twofold life!

To Adam Lindsay Gordon, I who laid
Two years ago on Lionel Michael's grave
A tender leaf of my regard; yea, I
Who culled a garland from the flowers of song
To place where Harpur sleeps; I, left alone,
The sad disciple of a shining band
Now gone—to Adam Lindsay Gordon's name
I dedicate these lines; and if 'tis true
That, past the darkness of the grave, the soul
Becomes omniscient, then the bard may stoop
From his high seat to take the offering,
And read it with a sigh for human friends,
In human bonds, and grey with human griefs.

And having wove and proffered this poor wreath,
I stand today as lone as he who saw
At nightfall, through the glimmering moony mist,
The last of Arthur on the wailing mere,
And strained in vain to hear the going voice.

IN MEMORIAM

MARCUS CLARKE

The nightwind sobs on cliffs austere
    Where gleams by fits the wintry star;
And in the wild dumb woods I hear
    A moaning harbour bar.

The branch and leaf are very still;
    But now the great grave dark has grown,
The torrent in the harsh sea-hill
    Sends forth a deeper tone.

Some sad, faint voice is far above;
    And many things I dream, it saith,
Of home made beautiful by Love
    And sanctified by Death.

I cannot catch its perfect phrase;
    But ah, the touching words to me
Bring back the lights of other days—
    The friends that used to be.

Here, sitting by a dying flame,
    I cannot choose but think with grief
Of Harpur, whose unhappy name
    Is as an autumn leaf.

And domed by purer depths of blue,
    Afar from folds of forest dark,
I see the eyes that once I knew—
    The eyes of Marcus Clarke.

Their clear, bright beauty shines a space;
    But sunny dreams in shadows end,
The sods have hid the faded face
    Of my heroic friend.

He sleeps where winds of evening pass—
    Where water songs are soft and low—
Upon his grave the tender grass
    Has not had time to grow.

69

G

Few knew the cross he had to bear,
    And moan beneath from day to day.
His were the bitter hours that wear
    The human heart away.

The laurels in the pit were won:
    He had to take the lot austere
That ever seems to wait upon
    The man of letters here.

His soul was self-withdrawn. He made
    A secret of the bitter life
Of struggle in inclement shade
    For helpless child and wife.

He toiled for Love, unwatched, unseen,
    And fought his troubles band by band,
Till, like a friend of gentle mien,
    Death took him by the hand.

He rests in peace! No grasping thief
    Of hope and health can steal away
The beauty of the flower and leaf
    Upon his tomb today.

The fragrant wood winds sing above
    Where gleams the grace of willow fair;
And often kneels a mournful Love
    To plant a blossom there.

So let him sleep, whose life was hard!
    And may they place, beyond the wave,
This tender rose of my regard
    Upon his tranquil grave.

IN MEMORIAM

DANIEL HENRY DENIEHY*

Take the harp, but very softly for our brother touch the strings:
Wind and wood shall help to wail him, waves and mournful moun-
tain-springs.
Take the harp, but very softly, for the friend who grew so old
Through the hours we would not hear of—nights we would not fain
behold!
Other voices, sweeter voices, shall lament him year by year,
Though the morning finds us lonely, though we sit and marvel here:
Marvel much while Summer cometh trammelled with November
wheat,
Gold about her forehead gleaming, green and gold about her feet;
Yea, and while the land is dark with plover, gull, and gloomy glede,
Where the cold swift songs of Winter fill the interlucent reed.

Yet my harp, and O, my fathers, never look for Sorrow's lay,
Making life a mighty darkness in the patient noon of day;
Since he resteth whom we loved so, out beyond these fleeting seas,
Blowing clouds, and restless regions paved with old perplexities,
In a land where thunder breaks not, in a place unknown of snow,
Where the rain is mute for ever, where the wild winds never go:
Home of far-forgotten phantoms—genii of our peaceful prime,
Shining by perpetual waters past the ways of Change and Time:
Haven of the harried spirit, where it folds its wearied wings,
Turns its face and sleeps a sleep with deep forgetfulness of things.

His should be a grave by mountains, in a cool and thick-mossed lea,
With the lone creek falling past it—falling ever to the sea.
His should be a grave by waters, by a bright and broad lagoon,
Making steadfast splendours hallowed of the quiet-shining moon.
There the elves of many forests—wandering winds and flying lights—
Born of green, of happy mornings, dear to yellow summer nights,

---

* Deniehy, lawyer and politician, brilliant as orator, journalist, and literary
critic, died destitute in 1865. He was a friend of Kendall's in the early
sixties, and encouraged the young poet. Kendall wrote feelingly of Deniehy's
tragedy in a letter to Harpur.

Full of dole for him that loved them, then might halt, and then might
   go,
Finding fathers of the people to their children speaking low—
Speaking low of one who, failing, suffered all the poet's pain,
Dying with the dead leaves round him—hopes which never grow
   again.

IN MEMORIAM

Archdeacon McEncroe*

A Father gone! In quiet skies
    The final ray died sweet and fair
Which closed his consecrated eyes
    As with a prayer.

Life left him like a faultless psalm
    That mounts and mingles with the stars;
And one more soul has reached the calm
    Past woes and wars.

So let them pass who live like him,
    Serene apostles with the faith
Which makes all Time a hallowed hymn
    And softens death!

We lingerers here will miss him much
    And all the grave specific grace
That touched, as with supernal touch,
    His gentle face.

His ways were light because he loved
    His suffering peers apart from sect;
A silent power by trouble proved
    And made elect.

In fiery times when Faith is faint,
    And Doubt has many words to say,
We'll often think how well this saint
    Kept fear away.

---

* Father John McEncroe, 1795-1868, born in Ireland, after service in America came to Sydney in 1832 as one of the first Roman Catholic chaplains. He was not only a leading figure in his Church for thirty-six years but also took a prominent part in reform of convict conditions, the agitation against revival of transportation, and land law reform. He won the affection and respect of all classes and denominations in the colony.

For, searching to the core of creeds,
    He found the sign that made him strong;
While we who sigh like seaside reeds,
    Do look and long.

The deep divinity which rests
    Forever at the root of things
Was shown to him who stood the tests
    Of sufferings.

And seeing beauty hid below
    The dust of dogmas evermore
He learned its speech, and came to know
    What Life is for.

The muffled bells, whose sound repeats
    The burden old that Time is swift,
The mournful faces in the streets
    All touch and lift—

All lift the soul to think how sweet
    Repose must lie upon the just
Who earned by love their right to sleep
    In holiest dust!

Who never turned aside for fear,
    Or murmured when in ways uncouth,
But lived and worked like Abdiels here
    For God and Truth.

JAMES LIONEL MICHAEL*

Be his rest the rest he sought:
    Calm and deep.
Let no wayward word or thought
    Vex his sleep.

Peace—the peace that no man knows—
    Now remains
Where the wasted woodwind blows,
    Wakes and wanes.

Latter leaves, in Autumn's breath,
    White and sere,
Sanctify the scholar's death,
    Lying here.

Soft surprises of the sun—
    Swift, serene—
O'er the mute grave-grasses run,
    Cold and green.

Wet and cold the hillwinds moan;
    Let them rave!
Love that takes a tender tone
    Lights his grave.

He who knew the friendless face
    Sorrows shew,
Often sought this quiet place
    Years ago.

---

* J. L. Michael, 1824-68, was a cultured scholar, a former friend of Millais and Ruskin in England, a brilliant conversationalist and a graceful lecturer. He treated Kendall as a younger brother, for some years was his cultural mentor, and took Kendall into his law office at Grafton. His death from drowning may have been due to suicide on account of financial and domestic troubles. His verse in *Songs Without Music*, 1857, and in the long autobiographical *John Cumberland*, 1860, was undistinguished.

One, too apt to faint and fail,
    Loved to stray
Here where water-shallows wail
    Day by day.

Care that lays her heavy hand
    On the best,
Bound him with an iron hand;
    Let him rest.

Life, that flieth like a tune,
    Left his eyes,
As an April afternoon
    Leaves the skies.

Peace is best! If life was hard
    Peace came next.
Thus the scholar, thus the bard,
    Lies unvext.

Safely housed at last from rack—
    Far from pain;
Who would wish to have him back?
    Back again?

Let the forms he loved so well
    Hover near;
Shine of hill and shade of dell,
    Year by year.

All the wilful waifs that make
    Beauty's face,
Let them sojourn for his sake
    Round this place.

Flying splendours, singing streams,
    Lutes and lights,
May they be as happy dreams:
    Sounds and sights;

So that Time to Love may say,
    "Wherefore weep?
Sweet is sleep at close of day!
    Death is sleep."

DEATH IN THE BUSH

THE GLEN OF ARRAWATTA

A sky of wind! And while these fitful gusts
Are beating round the windows in the cold,
With sullen sobs of rain, behold I shape
A Settler's story of the wild old times:
One told by campfires when the station-drays
Were housed and hidden, forty years ago;
While swarthy drivers smoked their pipes, and drew,
And crowded round the friendly-beaming flame
That lured the dingo howling from his caves
And brought sharp sudden feet about the brakes.

A tale of Love and Death! And shall I say
A tale of Love in Death; for all the patient eyes
That gathered darkness, watching for a son
And lover, never dreaming of the fate—
The fearful fate he met alone, unknown,
Within the ruthless Australasian wastes?
For in a far-off sultry summer rimmed
With thunder-cloud and red with forest-fires,
All day, by ways uncouth and ledges rude,
The wild men held upon a stranger's trail
Which ran against the rivers and athwart
The gorges of the deep blue western hills.

And when a cloudy sunset, like the flame
In windy evenings on the Plains of Thirst
Beyond the dead banks of the far Barcoo,
Lay heavy down the topmost peaks, they came
With pent-in breath and stealthy steps, and crouched
Like snakes amongst the tussocks, till the Night
Had covered face from face and thrown the gloom
Of many shadows on the front of things.

There, in the shelter of a nameless Glen
Fenced round by cedars and the tangled growths
Of blackwood stained with brown and shot with grey,
The jaded white man built his fire, and turned

His horse adrift amongst the water-pools
That trickled underneath the yellow leaves
And made a pleasant murmur, like the brooks
Of England through the sweet autumnal noons.

Then, after he had slaked his thirst, and used
The forest fare, for which a healthful day
Of mountain-life had brought a zest, he took
His axe, and shaped with boughs and wattle-forks
A wurley, fashioned like a bushman's roof:
A door brought out athwart the strenuous flame:
The back thatched in against a rising wind.

And while the sturdy hatchet filled the clifts
With sounds unknown, the immemorial haunts
Of echoes sent their lonely dwellers forth
Which lived a life of wonder: flying round
And round the glen—what time the kangaroo
Leapt from his lair and huddled with the bats—
Far-scattering down the wildly-startled fells.

Then came the doleful owl; and evermore
The bleak morass gave out the bittern's call;
The plover's cry; and many a fitful wail
Of chilly omen, falling on the ear
Like those cold flaws of wind that come and go
An hour before the break of day.

                                                    Anon
The stranger held from toil, and, settling down,
He drew rough solace from his well-filled pipe
And smoked into the night: revolving there
The primal questions of a squatter's life;
For in the flats, a short day's journey past
His present camp, his station yards were kept
With many a lodge and paddock jutting forth
Across the heart of unnamed prairie-lands,
Now loud with bleating and the cattle bells,
And misty with the hutfire's daily smoke.

Widespreading flats, and western spurs of hills
That dipped to plains of dim perpetual blue;
Bald summits set against the thunder-heaps;

And slopes be-hacked and crushed by battling kine!
Where now the furious tumult of their feet
Gives back the dust and up from glen and brake
Evokes fierce clamour, and becomes indeed
A token of the squatter's daring life,
Which growing inland—growing year by year,
Doth set us thinking in these latter days,
And makes one ponder of the lonely lands
Beyond the lonely tracks of Burke and Wills,
Where, when the wandering Stuart fixed his camps
In central wastes afar from any home
Or haunt of man, and in the changeless midst
Of sullen deserts and the footless miles
Of sultry silence, all the ways about
Grew strangely vocal and a marvellous noise
Became the wonder of the waxing glooms.

Now after Darkness, like a mighty spell
Amongst the hills and dim dispeopled dells,
Had brought a stillness to the soul of things,
It came to pass that, from the secret depths
Of dripping gorges, many a runnel-voice
Came, mellowed with the silence, and remained
About the caves, a sweet though alien sound:
Now rising ever, like a fervent flute
In moony evenings, when the theme is love:
Now falling, as ye hear the Sunday bells
While hastening fieldward from the gleaming town.

Then fell a softer mood; and Memory paused
With faithful Love, amidst the sainted shrines
Of Youth and Passion in the valleys past
Of dear delights which never grow again.
And if the stranger (who had left behind
Far anxious homesteads in a wave-swept isle
To face a fierce sea-circle day by day,
And hear at night the dark Atlantic's moan)
Now took a hope and planned a swift return,
With wealth and health and with a youth unspent,
To those sweet ones that stayed with Want at home,
Say *who* shall blame him—though the years are long,
And Life is hard, and waiting makes the heart grow old?

Thus passed the time until the Moon serene
Stood over high dominion like a dream
Of Peace: within the white-transfigured woods;
And o'er the vast dew-dripping wilderness
Of slopes illumined with her silent fires.
Then, far beyond the home of pale red leaves
And silver sluices and the shining stems
Of runnel-blooms, the dreamy wanderer saw,
The wilder for the vision of the moon,
Stark desolations and a waste of plain
All smit by flame and broken with the storms:
Black ghosts of trees, and sapless trunks that stood
Harsh hollow channels of the fiery noise
Which ran from bole to bole a year before,
And grew with ruin, and was like, indeed,
The roar of mighty winds with wintering streams
That foam about the limits of the land,
And mix their swiftness with the flying seas.

Now, when the man had turned his face about
To take his rest, behold the gem-like eyes
Of ambushed wild things stared from bole and brake
With dumb amaze and faint-recurring glance
And fear anon that drove them down the brush;
While from his den the dingo, like a scout
In sheltered ways, crept out and cowered near
To sniff the tokens of the stranger's feast
And marvel at the shadows of the flame.

But, under screen of glittering leaf and vine,
The man grew silent, and a fitful sleep
Veiled all the strange surroundings; and, while Night
In white mid-heaven shone with star by star,
A swift wild spirit from the sphere of Dreams
Slid down and took the weary wanderer's soul
Far back, away from wood and singing stream
To where the Past with all its varied hues
Of beam and shadow rose and lived again.
Yea, when the subtle spectre waved its wand,
The shining life that left the body saw
The vivid features of a bygone storm:

Fierce horns of land and gleaming crescents shot
With fire-like foam; and bends of moaning bay
Sad with the voice of shipwreck, and the cry
Of strong sea-eagle hunting for the drowned.
Ah! then before the mournful spirit's view
Passed bold New Zealand girt by lordly hills
That live with highest thunder and the snow
And speak with God and Morning in the flame,
And, where the teeth of reef by reef shone out
In straits of roaring water, lo, the hull
Of ruined vessel reeling in the surf
Was seen in that weird dream; and then there came
A hand of change that drew the sea away
And hushed the lips of tempest: then the soul
Beheld an English meadow starred with flowers
And cool with deep green grasses where the kine
Stand dreaming in a tender April sun.
And, past a border fragrant with the breath
Of Sussex blooms, the life outside the flesh
Saw at a leafy window one who sat
In all the glory of her golden hair
With sweet blue eyes that strained towards the wave
At watch for him whose step in Northern zones
On Northern lawns was never heard again.

So came and went the visions till a voice
Of beauty sang the soul into its shell
And lulled its life into a perfect sleep.
Thereafter grew the wind; and chafing depths
In distant waters sent a troubled cry
Across the slumb'rous Forest; and the chill
Of coming rain was on the sleeper's brow
When, flat as reptiles hutted in the scrub,
A deadly crescent crawled to where he lay—
A band of fierce fantastic savages
That, starting naked round the faded fire,
With sudden spears and swift terrific yells,
Came bounding wildly at the white man's head,
And faced him, staring like a dream of Hell!

Here let me pass! I would not stay to tell
Of hopeless struggles under crushing blows;
Of how the surging fiends with thickening strokes

Howled round the Stranger till they drained his strength;
How Love and Life stood face to face with Hate
And Death; and then how Death was left alone
With Night and Silence in the sobbing rains.

Ah! while within the folds of dumb dank hills
Of dark Orara lined with wailing oaks
The dying traveller moaned a touching prayer,
The greyhaired fathers of a Saxon home
Sat by their Sussex fire, what time the board
Was stacked with generous fare of meat and drink;
And these white elders talked into the night
With cheerful voices of the sturdy son
Who left their thresholds seven years before,
And crossed the seas, and under other skies
Found Fortune's fruit; and now was on his way
(So thought the fathers) to his friends again.

But after many moons, the searchers found
The body mouldering in the mouldering dell
Amidst the fungi and the bleaching leaves,
And buried it; and raised a stony mound
Which took the mosses: then the place became
The haunt of fearful legends, and the lair
Of bats and adders.

            There he lies and sleeps
From year to year: in soft Australian nights;
And through the furnaced noons; and in the times
Of wind and wet! yet never mourner comes
To drop upon that grave the Christian's tear
Or pluck the foul dank weeds of death away.

But while the English Autumn filled her lap
With faded gold, and while the reapers cooled
Their flame-red faces in the clover grass,
They looked for him at home; and when the frost
Had made a silence in the morning lanes,
And cooped the farmers by December fires,
They looked for him at home: and through the days
Which brought about the million-coloured Spring
With moon-like splendours in the garden plots,
They looked for him at home: while Summer danced,

A shining singer, through the tasselled corn,
They looked for him at home. From sun to sun
They waited. Season after season went,
And Memory wept upon the lonely moors,
And Hope grew voiceless, and the watchers passed,
Like shadows, one by one, away.

                                        And he,
Whose fate was hidden under forest leaves,
And in the darkness of untrodden dells,
Became a marvel. Often by the hearths
In winter nights, and when the wind was wild
Outside the casements, children heard the tale
Of how he left their native vales behind
(Where he had been a child himself) to shape
New fortunes for his father's fallen house;
Of how he struggled—how his name became,
By fine devotion and unselfish zeal,
A name of beauty in a selfish land;
And then, of how the aching hours went by
With patient listeners praying for the step
Which never crossed the floor again. So passed
The tale to children; but the bitter end
Remained a wonder, like the unknown grave
Alone with God and Silence in the hills.

LEICHHARDT

Lordly harp, by lordly Master wakened from majestic sleep,
Yet shall speak and yet shall sing the words which make the fathers
    weep—
Voice surpassing human voices—high unearthly harmony—
Yet shall tell the tale of hero, in exalted years to be!
In the ranges, by the rivers, on the uplands, down the dells,
Where the sound of wind and wave is—where the mountain anthem
    swells,
Yet shall float the song of lustre, sweet with tears and fair with flame,
Shining with a theme of beauty—holy with our Leichhardt's name!
Name of him who faced for Science thirsty tracts of bitter glow—
Lurid lands that no one knows of—two and thirty years ago.

Born by hills of hard grey weather, far beyond the northern seas,
German mountains were his "sponsors", and his mates were German
    trees.
Grandeur of the old-world forests passed into his radiant soul,
With the song of stormy crescents where the mighty waters roll.
Thus he came to be a brother of the river and the wood—
Thus the leaf, the bird, the blossom, grew a gracious sisterhood!
Nature led him to her children in a space of light divine—
Kneeling down, he said—"My Mother, let me be as one of thine!"
So she took him—thence she loved him—lodged him in her home
    of dreams:
Taught him what the trees were saying, schooled him in the speech
    of streams.

For her sake he crossed the waters—loving her, he left the place
Hallowed by his father's ashes and his human mother's face—
Passed the seas and entered temples domed by skies of deathless
    beam—
Walled about by hills majestic—stately spires and peaks supreme!
Here he found a larger beauty—here the lovely lights were new
On the slopes of many flowers, down the gold green dells of dew.
In the great august cathedral of his holy Lady, he
Daily worshipped at her altars, nightly bent the reverent knee—
Heard the hymns of night and morning, learned the psalm of soli-
    tudes:
Knew that God was very near him—felt His Presence in the woods!

But the starry angel, Science, from the home of glittering wings,
Came one day and talked to Nature by melodious mountain springs—
"Let thy son be mine," she pleaded, "lend him for a space," she said,
"So that he may earn the laurels I have woven for his head!"
And the Lady, Nature, listened; and she took her loyal son
From the banks of moss and myrtle—led him to the Shining One!
Filled his lordly soul with gladness—told him of a spacious zone
Eye of man had never looked at—human foot had never known;
Then the angel, Science, beckoned, and he knelt and whispered low—
"I will follow where you lead me"—two and thirty years ago.

On the tracts of thirst and furnace—on the dumb, blind burning plain
Where the red earth gapes for moisture and the wan leaves hiss for
    rain,
In a land of dry fierce thunder, did he ever pause and dream
Of the cool green German valley and the singing German stream?
When the sun was as a menace glaring from a sky of brass,
Did he ever rest, in visions, on a lap of German grass?
Past the waste of thorny terrors, did he reach a sphere of rills
In a region yet untravelled, ringed by fair untrodden hills?
Was the spot where last he rested pleasant as an old-world lea?
Did the sweet winds come and lull him with the music of the sea?

Let us dream so—let us hope so! Haply, in a cool green glade,
Far beyond the zone of furnace, Leichhardt's sacred shell was laid!
Haply in some leafy valley, underneath blue gracious skies,
In the sound of mountain water, the heroic traveller lies!
Down a dell of dewy myrtle, where the light is soft and green,
And a month, like English April, sits—an immemorial queen,
Let us think that he is resting—think that by a radiant grave
Ever come the songs of forest and the voices of the wave!
Thus we want our sons to find him—find him under floral bowers,
Sleeping by the trees he loved so—covered with his darling flowers!

THE HUT BY THE BLACK SWAMP

Now comes the fierce North-Easter, bound
　　About with cloud and racks of rain;
And dry dead leaves go whirling round
　　　In rings of dust, and sigh like Pain
　　　Across the plain.

Now Twilight, with a shadowy hand
　　Of wild dominionship, doth keep
Strong hold of hollow straits of land;
　　　And watery sounds are loud and deep
　　　By gap and steep.

Keen fitful gusts that fly before
　　The wings of Storm when Day hath shut
Its eyes on mountains, flaw by flaw,
　　　Fleet down by whistling boxtree-butt
　　　Against the Hut.

And ringed and girt with lurid pomp
　　Far eastern cliffs start up and take
Thick steaming vapours from a swamp
　　　That lieth like a great blind lake
　　　Of face opaque.

The moss that like a tender grief
　　About an English ruin clings—
What time the wan autumnal leaf
　　　Faints after many wanderings
　　　On windy wings—

That gracious growth whose quiet green
　　Is as a love in days austere,
Was never seen—hath never been
　　　On slab or roof, deserted here
　　　For many a year.

Nor comes the bird whose speech is song—
　　Whose songs are silvery syllables
That unto glimmering woods belong,
　　　And deep meandering mountain-dells
　　　By yellow wells.

But rather here the wild dog halts,
    And lifts the paw, and looks, and howls;
And here, in ruined forest-vaults,
    Abide dim, dark, death-featured owls,
        Like monks in cowls.

Across this Hut the nettle runs;
    And livid adders make their lair
In corners dank from lack of suns;
    And out of fetid furrows stare
        The growths that scare.

Here Summer's grasp of fire is laid
    On bark and slabs that rot and breed
Squat ugly things of deadly shade—
    The scorpion, and the spiteful seed
        Of centipede.

Unhallowed thunders harsh and dry,
    And flaming noontides mute with heat,
Beneath the breathless, brazen sky,
    Upon these rifted rafters beat
        With torrid feet.

And night by night, the fitful gale
    Doth carry past the bittern's boom,
The dingo's yell, the plover's wail,
    While lumbering shadows start, and loom,
        And hiss through gloom.

No sign of grace—no hope of green,
    Cool-blossomed seasons marks the spot;
But, chained to iron doom, I ween,
    'Tis left, like skeleton, to rot
        Where ruth is not.

For on this Hut hath Murder writ
    With bloody fingers hellish things;
And God will never visit it
    With flower or leaf of sweet-faced Springs,
        Or gentle wings.

CHRISTMAS CREEK

Phantom streams were in the distance—mocking lights of lake and
    pool—
Ghosts of trees of soft green lustre—groves of shadows deep and cool!
Yea, some devil ran before them changing skies of brass to blue:
Setting bloom where curse is planted—where a grass-blade never
    grew.
Six there were, and high above them glared a wild and wizened sun,
Ninety leagues from where the waters of the singing valleys run.
There before them—there behind them, was the great stark stubborn
    Plain
Where the dry winds hiss for ever and the blind earth moans for rain!
Ringed about by tracts of furnace, ninety leagues from stream and
    tree,
Six there were with wasted faces, working northwards to the sea!

    ·   ·   ·   ·   ·

Ah, the bitter hopeless Desert! Here these broken human wrecks
Trod the wilds where sand of fire is with the spiteful spinifex!
Toiled through spheres that no bird knows of, where with fiery
    emphasis
Hell hath stamped its awful mintmark deep on everything that is!
Toiled and thirsted, strove and suffered! *This* was where December's
    breath
As a wind of smiting flame is on weird haggard wastes of Death!
This was where a withered moan is, and the gleam of weak wan star,
And a thunder full of menace sends its mighty voices far!
This was where black execrations, from some dark Tribunal hurled,
Set the brand of curse on all things in the morning of the World!

    ·   ·   ·   ·   ·

One man yielded—then another—then a lad of nineteen years
Reeled and fell with English rivers singing softly in his ears.
English grasses started round him—then the grace of Sussex lea
Came and touched him with the beauty of a green land by the sea!
Old-world faces thronged about him—old-world voices spoke to him;
But his speech was like a whisper, and his eyes were very dim.
In a dream of golden evening beaming on a quiet strand,
Lay the stranger till a bright One came and took him by the hand.
England vanished, died the voices! but he heard a holier tone,
And an angel that we know not led him to the Lands unknown!

    ·   ·   ·   ·   ·

Six there were, but three were taken! Three were left to struggle still;
But against the red horizon flamed a horn of brindled hill!
But beyond the northern skyline, past a wall of steep austere,
Lay the land of light and coolness in an April-coloured year!
"Courage, brothers," cried the leader, "on the slope of yonder peak
There are tracts of herb and shadow and the channels of the creek!"
So they made one last great effort—haled their beasts through brake
    and briar—
Set their feet on spurs of furnace—grappled spikes and crags of fire—
Fought the stubborn mountain forces—smote down naked natural
    powers,
Till they gazed from thrones of Morning on a sphere of streams and
    flowers.

.   .   .   .   .

Out behind them was the desert glaring like a sea of brass!
Here before them were the valleys fair with moonlight-coloured
    grass!
At their backs were haggard wastelands bickering in a wicked blaze!
In their faces beamed the waters marching down melodious ways!
Touching was the cool soft lustre over laps of lawn and lea;
And majestic was the great road Morning made across the sea.
On the sacred day of Christmas, after seven months of grief,
Rested three of six who started, on a bank of moss and leaf—
Rested by a running river, in a hushed, a holy week;
And they named the stream that saved them—named it fitly—"Christ-
    mas Creek".

GHOST GLEN

"Shut your ears, stranger, or turn from Ghost Glen now,
For the paths are grown over; untrodden by men now—
Shut your ears, stranger!" saith the grey mother, crooning
Her sorcery Runic, when sets the half moon in!

Tonight the North-Easter goes travelling slowly,
But it never stoops down to that Hollow unholy—
Tonight it rolls loud on the ridges red-litten,
But it *cannot* abide in that Forest sin-smitten!

For over the pitfall the moondew is thawing,
And, with never a body, two shadows stand sawing!
The wraiths of two sawyers (*step under and under*),
Who did a foul murder, and were blackened with thunder!

Whenever the storm-wind comes driven and driving,
Through the blood-spattered timber you may see the saw striving—
You may see the saw heaving, and falling, and heaving,
Whenever the sea-creek is chafing and grieving!

And across a burnt body, as black as an adder,
Sits the sprite of a sheep-dog! was ever sight sadder!
For as the dry thunder splits louder and faster,
This sprite of a sheep-dog howls for his master!

"Oh! count your beads deftly," saith the grey mother, crooning
Her sorcery Runic, when sets the half moon in!
And well may she mutter, for the dark hollow laughter
You will hear in the sawpits, and the bloody logs after!

Ay, count your beads deftly, and keep your ways wary,
For the sake of the Saviour and sweet Mother Mary!
Pray for your peace in these perilous places,
And pray for the laying of horrible faces!

One starts with a forehead wrinkled and livid,
Aghast at the lightnings sudden and vivid!
One telleth with curses the gold that they drew there
(Ah! cross your breast humbly) from him whom they slew there!

The stranger who came from the loved—the romantic
Island that sleeps on the moaning Atlantic;
Leaving behind him a patient home yearning
For the steps in the distance, never returning;—

Who was left in the Forest, shrunken, and starkly
Burnt by his slayers (so men have said darkly):
With the half-crazy sheep-dog, who cowered beside there
And yelled at the silence, and marvelled, and died there!

Yea, cross your breast humbly, and hold your breath tightly,
Or fly for your life from those shadows unsightly;
From the set staring features (cold, and so young too!)
And the death on the lips that a mother hath clung to.

I tell you, the Bushman is braver than most men,
Who even in daylight doth go through the Ghost Glen!
Although in that Hollow, unholy and lonely,
He sees the dank sawpits and bloody logs only!

COORANBEAN

Years fifty, and seven to boot, have smitten the children of men
Since sound of a voice or a foot came out of the head of that Glen:
The brand of black devil is there—an evil wind moaneth around—
There is doom, there is death in the air: a curse groweth up from the
    ground!
No noise of the axe or the saw in that Hollow unholy is heard:
No fall of the hoof or the paw—no whirr of the wing of the bird;
But a grey mother down by the sea, as wan as the foam on the strait,
Has counted the beads on her knee these forty-nine winters and eight.

Whenever an elder is asked—a white-headed man of the woods—
Of the terrible mystery masked where the dark everlastingly broods,
Be sure he will turn to the bay with his back to the Glen in the range
And glide like a phantom away, with a countenance pallid with
    change.
From the line of dead timber that lies supine at the foot of the glade,
The fierce-featured eaglehawk flies—afraid as a dove is afraid;
But back in that wilderness dread are a fall and the forks of a ford—
Ah! pray and uncover your head, and lean like a child on the Lord.

A sinister fog at the wane—at the change of the moon cometh forth
Like an ominous ghost in the train of a bitter black storm of the North!
At the head of the Gully unknown, it hangs like a spirit of bale;
And the noise of a shriek and a groan strikes up in the gusts of the
    gale.
In the throat of a feculent pit is the beard of a bloody-red sedge;
And a foam like the foam of a fit sweats out of the lips of the ledge;
But down in the water of death, in the livid dead pool at the base—
Bow low with inaudible breath: beseech with the hands to the face!

A furlong of fetid black fen, with gelid green patches of pond,
Lies dumb by the horns of the Glen—at the gates of the Horror
    beyond;
And those who have looked on it tell of the terrible growths that are
    there—
The flowerage fostered by Hell—the blossoms that startle and scare;
If ever a wandering bird should light on Gehennas like this,

Be sure that a cry will be heard and the sound of the flat adder's hiss.
But, hard by the jaws of the bend is a ghastly Thing matted with
     moss—
Ah, Lord! be a Father, a Friend, for the sake of the Christ of the Cross!

Black Tom with the sinews of five—that never a hangman could
     hang—
In the days of the shackle and gyve, broke loose from the guards of the
     gang.
Thereafter, for seasons a score, this devil prowled under the ban:
A mate of red talon and paw—a wolf in the shape of a man.
But, ringed by ineffable fire, in a thunder and wind of the North,
The sword of Omnipotent ire—the bolt of high heaven went forth!
But, wan as the sorrowful foam, a grey mother waits by the sea
For the boys that have never come home these fifty-four winters and
     three.

From the folds of the forested hills there are ravelled and roundabout
     tracks,
Because of the terror that fills the strong-handed men of the axe!
Of the workers away in the range, there is none that will wait for the
     night
When the storm-stricken moon is in change, and the sinister fog is in
     sight.
And later and deep in the dark, when the bitter wind whistles about,
There is never a howl or a bark from the dog in the kennel without;
But the white fathers fasten the door, and often and often they start
At a sound like a foot on the floor and a touch like a hand on the heart.

ON THE PAROO

As when the strong stream of a wintering sea
Rolls round our coast, with bodeful breaks of storm,
And swift salt rain, and bitter wind that saith
Wild things and woeful of the White South Land
Alone with God and Silence in the cold—
As when this cometh, men from dripping doors
Look forth, and shudder for the mariners
Abroad, so we for absent brothers looked
In days of drought, and when the flying floods
Swept boundless: roaring down the bald, black, plains
Beyond the farthest spur of western hills.

For where the Barwan cuts a rotten land,
Or lies unshaken, like a great blind creek,
Between hot mouldering banks, it came to this,
All in a time of short and thirsty sighs,
That thirty rainless months had left the pools
And grass as dry as ashes: then it was
Our kinsman started for the lone Paroo,
From point to point, with patient strivings, sheer
Across the horrors of the windless downs,
Blue-gleaming like a sea of molten steel.

But never drought had broke them: never flood
Had quenched them: they with mighty youth and health,
And thews and sinews knotted like the trees—
They, like the children of the native woods,
Could stem the strenuous waters, or outlive
The crimson days and dull dead nights of thirst
Like camels! yet of what avail was strength
Alone to them—though it was like the rocks
On stormy mountains—in the bloody time
When fierce sleep caught them in the camps at rest,
And violent darkness gripped the life in them
And whelmed them, as an eagle unawares
Is whelmed and slaughtered in a sudden snare.

All murdered by the blacks! smit while they lay
In silver dreams, and with the far faint fall
Of many waters breaking on their sleep!
Yea, in the tracts unknown of any man
Save savages—the dim-discovered ways
Of footless silence or unhappy winds—
The wild men came upon them, like a fire
Of desert thunder; and the fine firm lips
That touched a mother's lips a year before,
And hands that knew a dearer hand than life,
Were hewn like sacrifice before the stars,
And left with hooting owls, and blowing clouds,
And falling leaves, and solitary wings!

Ay, you may see their graves—you who have toiled,
And tripped, and thirsted, like these men of ours;
For verily I say that *not* so deep
Their bones are that the scattered drift and dust
Of gusty days will never leave them bare.
O dear, dead, bleaching bones! I know of those
Who have the wild strong will to go and sit
Outside all things with you, and keep the ways
Aloof from bats, and snakes, and trampling feet
That smite your peace and theirs—who have the heart
Without the lusty limbs to face the fire,
And moonless midnights, and to be indeed,
For very sorrow, like a moaning wind
In wintry forests with perpetual rain.

Because of this—because of sisters left
With desperate purpose and dishevelled hair,
And broken breath, and sweetness quenched in tears—
Because of swifter silver for the head,
And furrows for the face—because of these
That should have come with Age, that come with Pain,
O Master! Father! sitting where our eyes
Are tired of looking, say for once are we—
Are *we* to set our lips with weary smiles
Before the bitterness of Life and Death,
And call it honey, while we bear away
A taste like wormwood?

Turn thyself, and sing—
Sing, Son of Sorrow! Is there any gain
For breaking of the loins, for melting eyes,
And knees as weak as water? any peace,
Or hope, for casual breath, and labouring lips,
For clapping of the palms, and sharper sighs
Than frost; or any light to come for those
Who stand and mumble in the alien streets
With heads as grey as Winter? any balm
For pleading women, and the love that knows
Of nothing left to love?

They sleep a sleep
Unknown of dreams, these darling friends of ours.
And *we* who taste the core of many tales
Of tribulation—*we* whose lives are salt
With tears indeed—we therefore hide our eyes
And weep in secret lest our grief should risk
The rest that hath no hurt from daily racks
Of fiery clouds and immemorial rains.

A DEATH IN THE BUSH

The hut was built of bark and shrunken slabs
That wore the marks of many rains, and showed
Dry flaws, wherein had crept and nestled rot.
Moreover, round the bases of the bark
Were left the tracks of flying forest-fires,
As you may see them on the lower bole
Of every elder of the native woods.

For, ere the early settlers came and stocked
These wilds with sheep and kine, the grasses grew
So that they took the passing pilgrim in,
And whelmed him, like a running sea, from sight.

And therefore, through the fiercer summer months,
While all the swamps were rotten—while the flats
Were baked and broken; when the clayey rifts
Yawned wide, half-choked with drifted herbage past,
Spontaneous flames would burst from thence, and race
Across the prairies all day long.

                                        At night
The winds were up, and then with fourfold speed,
A harsh gigantic growth of smoke and fire
Would roar along the bottoms, in the wake
Of fainting flocks of parrots, wallaroos,
And 'wildered wild things, scattering right and left,
For safety vague, throughout the general gloom.

Anon, the nearer hill-side growing trees
Would take the surges; thus, from bough to bough,
Was borne the flaming terror! Bole and spire,
Rank after rank, now pillared, ringed, and rolled
In blinding blaze, stood out against the dead
Down-smothered dark, for fifty leagues away.

For fifty leagues! and when the winds were strong,
For fifty more! But, in the olden time,
These fires were counted as the harbingers
Of life-essential storms; since out of smoke

And heat there came across the midnight ways
Abundant comfort, with upgathered clouds,
And runnels babbling of a plenteous fall.

So comes the Southern gale at evenfall
(The swift "brickfielder" of the local folk)
About the streets of Sydney, when the dust
Lies burnt on glaring windows, and the men
Look forth from doors of drouth, and drink the change
With thirsty haste and that most thankful cry
Of, "here it is—the cool, bright, blessed rain!"

The hut, I say, was built of bark and slabs,
And stood, the centre of a clearing, hemmed
By hurdle-years, and ancients of the blacks:
These moped about their lazy fires, and sang
Wild ditties of the old days, with a sound
Of sorrow, like an everlasting wind,
Which mingled with the echoes of the noon,
And moaned amongst the noises of the night.

From thence a cattle-track, with link to link,
Ran off against the fishpools, to the gap,
Which sets you face to face with gleaming miles
Of broad Orara, winding in amongst
Black, barren ridges, where the nether spurs
Are fenced about by cotton-scrub, and grass
Blue-bitten with the salt of many droughts.

'Twas here the shepherd housed him every night,
And faced the prospect like a patient soul;
Borne up by some vague hope of better days,
And God's fine blessing in his faithful wife;
Until the humour of his malady
Took cunning changes from the good to bad,
And laid him lastly on a bed of death.

Two months thereafter, when the summer heat
Had roused the serpent from his rotten lair,
And made a noise of locusts in the boughs,
It came to this, that, as the blood-red sun
Of one fierce day of many slanted down

Obliquely past the nether jags of peaks
And gulfs of mist, the tardy night came vexed
By belted clouds, and scuds that wheeled and whirled
To left and right about the brazen clifts
Of ridges, rigid with a leaden gloom.

Then took the cattle to the forest camps
With vacant terror, and the hustled sheep
Stood dumb against the hurdles, even like
A fallen patch of shadowed mountain snow;
And ever through the curlew's call afar
The storm grew on, while round the stinted slabs
Sharp snaps and hisses came, and went, and came,
The huddled tokens of a mighty blast
Which ran with an exceeding bitter cry
Across the tumbled fragments of the hills,
And through the sluices of the gorge and glen.

So, therefore, all about the shepherd's hut
That space was mute, save when the fastened dog,
Without a kennel, caught a passing glimpse
Of firelight moving through the lighted chinks;
For then he knew the hints of warmth within,
And stood, and set his great pathetic eyes,
In wind and wet, imploring to be loosed.

Not often now the watcher left the couch
Of him she watched; since, in his fitful sleep,
His lips would stir to wayward themes, and close
With bodeful catches. Once she moved away,
Half-deafened by terrific claps, and stooped,
And looked without; to see a pillar dim
Of gathered gusts and fiery rain.

                                        Anon,
The sick man woke, and, startled by the noise,
Stared round the room, with dull delirious sight,
At this wild thing and that; for, through his eyes,
The place took fearful shapes, and fever showed
Strange crosswise lights about his pillow-head.
He, catching there at some phantasmic help,
Sat upright on the bolster, with a cry
Of, "Where is Jesus?—it is bitter cold!"

And then, because the thundercalls outside
Were mixed for him with slanders of the Past,
He called his weeping wife by name, and said,
"Come closer, darling! we shall speed away
Across the seas, and seek some mountain home,
Shut in from liars, and the wicked words
That track us day and night, and night and day."

So waned the sad refrain. And those poor lips,
Whose latest phrases were for peace, grew mute,
And into everlasting silence passed.

As fares a swimmer who hath lost his breath
In 'wildering seas afar from any help—
Who, fronting Death, can never realize
The dreadful Presence, but is prone to clutch
At every weed upon the weltering wave;
So fared the watcher, poring o'er the last
Of him she loved, with dazed and stupid stare;
Half conscious of the sudden loss and lack
Of all that bound her life, but yet without
The power to take her mighty sorrow in.

Then came a patch or two of starry sky;
And through a reef of cloven thunder-cloud
The soft Moon looked: a patient face beyond
The fierce impatient shadows of the slopes,
And the harsh voices of the broken hills!
A patient face, and one which came and wrought
A lovely silence like a silver mist
Across the rainy relics of the storm.

For in the breaks and pauses of her light
The gale died out in gusts; yet, evermore
About the roof-tree, on the dripping eaves,
The damp wind loitered; and a fitful drift
Sloped through the silent curtains, and athwart
The dead.

       There, when the glare had dropped behind
A mighty ridge of gloom, the woman turned
And sat in darkness face to face with God,
And said—"I know," she said, "that Thou art wise;

That when we build and hope, and hope and build,
And see our best things fall, it comes to pass
For evermore that we must turn to Thee!
And therefore now, because I cannot find
The faintest token of Divinity
In this my latest sorrow, let Thy light
Inform mine eyes, so I may learn to look
On something past the sight which shuts, and blinds,
And seems to drive me wholly, Lord, from Thee."

Now waned the moon beyond complaining depths;
And, as the dawn looked forth from showery woods
(Whereon had dropt a hint of red and gold),
There went about the crooked cavern-eaves
Low flute-like echoes with a noise of wings
And waters flying down far-hidden fells.
Then might be seen the solitary owl,
Perched in the clefts; scared at the coming light,
And staring outward (like a sea-shelled thing
Chased to his cover by some bright fierce foe)
As at a monster in the middle waste.
At last the great kingfisher came and called
Across the hollows loud with early whips,
And lighted, laughing, on the shepherd's hut,
And roused the widow from a swoon like death.

This day, and after it was noised abroad,
By blacks, and straggling horsemen on the roads,
That he was dead "who had been sick so long",
There flocked a troop from far-surrounding runs
To see their neighbour and to bury him.
And men who had forgotten how to cry
(Rough flinty fellows of the native bush)
Now learned the bitter way, beholding there
The wasted shadow of an iron frame
Brought down so low by years of fearful pain;
And marking, too, the woman's gentle face,
And all the pathos in her moaned reply
Of "masters, we have lived in better days",
One stooped—a stockman from the nearer hills—
To loose his wallet-strings, from whence he took

A bag of tea, and laid it on her lap;
Then, sobbing, "God will help you, missus, yet",
He sought his horse with most bewildered eyes,
And, spurring swiftly, galloped down the glen.

Where black Orara nightly chafes his brink,
Midway between lamenting lines of oak
And Warra's gap, the shepherd's grave was built.
And there the wild-dog pauses, in the midst
Of moonless watches: howling through the gloom
At hopeless shadows flitting to and fro,
What time the East Wind hums his darkest hymn,
And rains beat heavy on the ruined leaf.

There, while the Autumn in the cedar trees
Sat cooped about by cloudy evergreens,
The widow sojourned on the silent road,
And mutely faced the barren mound, and plucked
A straggling shrub from thence, and passed away,
Heart-broken on to Sydney; where she took
Her passage, in an English vessel bound
To London, for her home of other years.

At rest! not near, with Sorrow on his grave,
And roses quickened into beauty—wrapt
In all the pathos of perennial bloom;
But far from these, beneath the fretful clay
Of lands within the lone perpetual cry
Of hermit plovers and the night-like oaks,
All moaning for the peace which never comes.

At rest! And she who sits and waits behind
Is in the shadows; but her faith is sure,
And *one* fine promise of the coming days
Is breaking, like a blessed morning, far
On hills "that slope through darkness up to God".

FROM ITHACA AND GILBOA

SYRINX[*]

A heap of low dark rocky coast
    Unknown to foot or feather!
A sea-voice moaning like a ghost;
    And fits of fiery weather!

The flying Syrinx turned and sped
    By dim mysterious hollows,
Where night is black, and day is red,
    And frost the fire-wind follows!

Strong heavy footfalls in the wake,
    Came up with flights of water:
The gods were mournful for the sake
    Of Ladon's lovely daughter.

For when she came to spike and spine,
    Where reef and river gather,
Her feet were sore with shell and chine;
    She could not travel farther.

Across a naked strait of land,
    Blown sleet and surge were humming;
But trammelled with the shifting sand,
    She heard the monster coming!

A thing of hoofs, and horns, and lust!
    A gaunt goat-footed stranger!
She bowed her body in the dust,
    And called on Zeus to change her.

And called on Hermes fair and fleet,
    And her of hounds and quiver,
To hide her in the thickets sweet
    That sighed above the river.

---

[*] Syrinx, a nymph of Arcadia and daughter of the river Ladon, rejected the violent advances of the enamoured Pan. Her prayer to the gods for help was answered by her transformation into a reed called Syrinx. Pan, in turn, used these reeds to fashion his musical pipe.

So He that sits on flaming wheels,
    And rules the sea and thunder,
Caught up the satyr by the heels,
    And tore his skirts in sunder.

While Arcas of the glittering plumes
    Took Ladon's daughter lightly,
And set her in the gracious glooms
    That mix with moon-mist nightly.

And touched her lips with wild-flower wine;
    And changed her body slowly,
Till in soft reeds of song and shine
    Her life was hidden wholly.

THE VOYAGE OF TELEGONUS*

Ill fares it with the man whose lips are set
To bitter themes and words that spite the gods:
For, seeing how the son of Saturn sways
With eyes and ears for all, this one shall halt
As on hard hurtful hills; his days shall know
The plaintive front of Sorrow; level looks
With cries ill-favoured shall be dealt to him;
And *this* shall be that he may think of peace
As one might think of alienated lips
Of sweetness touched for once in kind warm dreams.
Yea, fathers of the high and holy face,
This soul thus sinning shall have cause to sob
"Ah, ah", for sleep, and space enough to learn
The wan wild Hyrie's aggregated song
That starts the dwellers in distorted heights,
With all the meaning of perpetual sighs
Heard in the mountained deserts of the world,
And where the green-haired waters glide between
The thin lank weeds and mallows of the marsh.

But thou to whom these things are like to shapes
That come of darkness—thou whose life slips past
Regarding rather these with mute fast mouth—
Hear none the less how fleet Telegonus,
The brass-clad hunter, first took oar and smote
Swift eastward-going seas, with face direct
For narrowing channels and the twofold coasts
Past Colchis and the fierce Symplegades
And utmost islands washed by streams unknown.

For in a time when Phasis whitened wide
And drove with violent waters blown of wind
Against the bare salt limits of the land,
It came to pass that, joined with Cytheraea,

---

* Telegonus, son of Ulysses and Circe, born and bred on Aeaea, journeyed to
Ithaca to see his father, but killed him not knowing who he was. Later he
married the widowed Penelope, and their son Italus gave his name to Italy.

The black-browed Ares, chafing for the wrong
Ulysses did him on the plains of Troy,
Set heart against the king; and when the storms
Sang high in thunder and the Thracian rain,
The god bethought him of a pale-mouthed priest
Of Thebae, kin to ancient Chariclo,
And of an omen which the prophet gave
That touched on Death and grief to Ithaca;
Then, knowing how a heavy-handed fate
Had laid itself on Circe's brass-clad son,
He pricked the hunter with a list that turned
All thoughts to travel and the seas remote;
But chiefly now he stirred Telegonus
To longings for his father's exiled face,
And dreams of rest and honey-hearted love,
And quiet death with much of funeral flame
Far in the mountains of a favoured land
Beyond the wars and wailings of the waves.

So past the ridges where the coast abrupt
Dips greyly westward, Circe's strong-armed son
Swept down the foam of sharp-divided straits
And faced the stress of opening seas. Sheer out
The Vessel drave; but three long moons the gale
Moaned round; and swift strong streams of fire revealed
The labouring rowers and the lightening surf,
Pale watchers deafened of sonorous storm,
And dripping decks and rents of ruined sails.
Yea, when the hollow ocean-driven ship
Wheeled sideways, like a chariot cloven through
In hard hot battle, and the night came up
Against strange headlands lying East and North,
Behold a black wild wind with death to all
Ran shoreward, charged with flame and thunder-smoke,
Which blew the waters into wastes of white
And broke the bark, as lightning breaks the pine;
Whereat the sea in fearful circles shewed
Unpitied faces turned from Zeus and light,
Wan swimmers wasted with their agony,
And hopeless eyes and moaning mouths of men.
But one held by the fragments of the wreck,
And Ares knew him for Telegonus,

Whom heavy-handed Fate had chained to deeds
Of dreadful note with sin beyond a name.
So, seeing this, the black-browed lord of war,
Arrayed about by Jove's authentic light,
Shot down amongst the shattered clouds and called
With mighty strain, betwixt the gaps of storm,
"Oceanus, Oceanus!" whereat
The surf sprang white, as when a keel divides
The gleaming centre of a gathered wave;
And, ringed with flakes of splendid fire of foam,
The son of Terra rose halfway and blew
The triple trumpet of the water-gods,
At which great winds fell back and all the sea
Grew dumb, as on the land a war-feast breaks
When deep sleep falls upon the souls of men.
Then Ares of the night-like brow made known
The brass-clad hunter of the facile feet
Hard clinging to the slippery logs of pine,
And told the omen to the hoary god
That touched on Death and grief to Ithaca;
Wherefore Oceanus with help of hand
Bore by the chin the warrior of the North,
A moaning mass, across the shallowing surge,
And cast him on the rocks of alien shores
Against a wintry morning shot with storm.

Hear also thou how mighty gods sustain
The men set out to work the ends of Fate
Which fill the world with tales of many tears,
And vex the sad face of Humanity;
Six days and nights the brass-clad chief abode
Pent up in caverns by the straightening seas,
And fed on ferns and limpets; but the dawn
Before the strong sun of the seventh, brought
A fume of fire and smells of savoury meat,
And much rejoicing, as from neighbouring feasts;
At which the hunter, seized with sudden lust,
Sprang up the crags, and, like a dream of Fear,
Leapt, shouting, at a huddled host of hinds
Amongst the fragments of their steaming food;
And, as the hoarse wood-wind in Autumn sweeps
To every zone the hissing latter leaves,

So, fleet Telegonus, by dint of spear
And strain of thunderous voice, did scatter these
East, South, and North: 'twas then the chief had rest,
Hard by the outer coast of Ithaca,
Unknown to him who ate the spoil and slept.
Nor stayed he hand thereafter; but, when noon
Burned dead on misty hills of stunted fir,
This man shook slumber from his limbs, and sped
Against hoar beaches and the kindled cliffs
Of falling waters; these he waded through,
Beholding past the forests of the West
A break of light, and homes of many men,
And shining corn, and flowers, and fruits of flowers;
Yea, seeing these, the facile-footed chief
Grasped by the knot the huge Aeaean lance,
And fell upon the farmers; wherefore they
Left hoe and plough, and crouched in heights remote
Companioned with the grey-winged fogs; but he
Made waste their fields and throve upon their toil—
As throve the boar, the fierce four-footed curse
Which Artemis did raise in Calydon
To make stern mouths wax white with foreign fear,
All in the wild beginning of the World.

So one went down and told Laertes' son
Of what the brass-clad stranger from the straits
Had worked in Ithaca: whereat the King
Rose, like a god, and called his mighty heir,
Telemachus, the wisest of the wise;
And these two, having counsel, strode without,
And armed them with the arms of warlike days—
The helm, the javelin, and the sun-like shield,
And glancing greaves and quivering stars of steel!
Yea, stern Ulysses, rusted not with rest,
But dread as Ares, gleaming on his car
Gave out the reins; and straightway all the lands
Were struck by noise of steed and shouts of men,
And furious dust, and splendid wheels of flame.
Meanwhile the hunter (starting from a sleep
In which the pieces of a broken dream
Had shown him Circe with most tearful face),
Caught at his spear, and stood, like one at bay

When Summer brings about Arcadian horns
And headlong horses mixt with maddened hounds;
Then huge Ulysses, like a fire of fight,
Sprang sideways on the flying car, and drave
Full at the brass-clad warrior of the North
His massive spear; but fleet Telegonus
Stooped from the death, but heard the speedy lance
Sing like a thin wind through the steaming air;
Yet he, dismayed not by the dreadful foe—
Unknown to him—dealt out his strength, and aimed
A strenuous stroke at great Laertes' son,
Which missed the shield, but bit through flesh and bone,
And drank the blood, and dragged the soul from thence!
So fell the King! and one cried "Ithaca!
Ah, Ithaca!" and turned his face and wept.
Then came another—wise Telemachus—
Who knelt beside the man of many days
And pored upon the face; but lo, the life
Was like bright water spilt in sands of thirst,
A wasted splendour swiftly drawn away.
Yet held he by the dead: he heeded not
The moaning warrior who had learnt his sin—
Who waited now, like one in lairs of pain,
Apart with darkness hungry for his fate;
For, had not wise Telemachus the lore
Which makes the pale-mouthed seer content to sleep
Amidst the desolations of the world?
So therefore he who knew Telegonus,
The child of Circe by Laertes' son,
Was set to be a scourge of Zeus, smote not
But rather sat with moody eyes, and mused,
And watched the dead. For who may brave the gods?

Yet, O my fathers, when the people came,
And brought the holy oils and perfect fire,
And built the pile, and sang the tales of Troy—
Of desperate travels in the olden time,
By shadowy mountains and the roaring sea,
Near windy sands and past the Thracian snows—
The man who crossed them all to see his sire,
And had a loyal heart to give the King,
Instead of blows—this man did little more
Than moan outside the fume of funeral rites,

All in a rushing twilight full of rain,
And clap his palms for sharper pains than swords.
Yea, when the night broke out against the flame,
And lonely noises loitered in the fens,
This man nor stirred nor slept, but lay at wait,
With fastened mouth. For who may brave the gods?

GALATEA*

A silver slope, a fall of firs, a league of gleaming grasses,
And fiery cones, and sultry spurs, and swarthy pits and passes!

.   .   .   .

The long-haired Cyclops bated breath, and bit his lip and hearkened,
And dug and dragged the stone of death, by ways that dipped and
darkened.

Across a tract of furnaced flints there came a wind of water,
From yellow banks with tender hints of Tethys' white-armed
daughter.

She sat amongst wild singing weeds, by beds of myrrh and môly;
And Acis made a flute of reeds, and drew its accents slowly;

And taught its spirit subtle sounds that leapt beyond suppression
And paused and panted on the bounds of fierce and fitful passion.

Then he who shaped the cunning tune, by keen desire made bolder,
Fell fainting, like a fervent noon, upon the sea-nymph's shoulder.

Sicilian suns had laid a dower of light and life about her:
Her beauty was a gracious flower—the heart fell dead without her.

"Ah, Galatê," said Polypheme, "I would that I could find thee
Some finest tone of hill or stream, wherewith to lull and bind thee!

"What lyre is left of marvellous range whose subtle strings, contain-
ing
Some note supreme, might catch and change, or set thy passion
waning?—

---

* Galatea, one of the Nereids, or sea-nymphs, daughter of Nereus and Doris.
Here she is represented as one of the Oceanids, a daughter of Oceanus and
Tethys. Loving the Sicilian shepherd Acis, she disdained the passion of Poly-
phemus, son of Neptune and Thoosa and king of the Cyclops in Sicily, where-
upon the jealous Cyclops killed Acis with a piece of broken rock. Galatea then
changed her dead lover to a fountain.

"Thy passion for the fair-haired youth whose fleet light feet perplex
    me
By ledges rude, on paths uncouth, and broken ways that vex me?

"Ah, turn to me! else violent sleep shall track the cunning lover;
And thou wilt wait and thou wilt weep when I his haunts discover."

But golden Galatea laughed, and Thôsa's son like thunder—
Brake through a rifty runnel shaft, and dashed its rocks asunder,

And poised the bulk, and hurled the stone, and crushed the hidden
    Acis,
And struck with sorrow drear and lone, the sweetest of all faces.

To Zeus, the mighty Father, she, with plaint and prayer, departed:
Then from fierce Aetna to the sea a fountained water started.

A lucent stream of lutes and lights. Cool haunt of flower and feather;
Whose silver days and yellow nights, made years of hallowed weather.

Here Galatea used to come, and rest beside the river;
Because, in faint soft blowing foam, her shepherd lived for ever.

OGYGES *

Stand out, swift-footed leaders of the horns,
And draw strong breath, and fill the hollowy cliff
With shocks of clamour,—let the chasm take
The noise of many trumpets, lest the hunt
Should die across the dim Aonian hills,
Nor break through thunder and the surf-white cave
That hems about the old-eyed Ogyges
And bars the sea-wind, rain-wind, and the sea!

Much fierce delight hath old-eyed Ogyges
(A hairless shadow in a lion's skin)
In tumult, and the gleam of flying spears,
And wild beasts vexed to death; "for", sayeth he,
"Here lying broken, do I count the days
For very trouble; being like the tree—
The many-wintered father of the trunks
On yonder ridges: wherefore it is well
To feel the dead blood kindling in my veins
At sound of boar or battle; yea to find
A sudden stir, like life, about my feet,
And tingling pulses through this frame of mine
What time the cold clear dayspring, like a bird
Afar off, settles on the frost-bound peaks,
And all the deep blue gorges, darkening down,
Are filled with men and dogs and furious dust!"

So in the time whereof thou weetest well—
The melancholy morning of the World—
He mopes or mumbles, sleeps or shouts for glee,
And shakes his sides—a cavern-hutted King!
But when the ouzel in the gaps at eve
Doth pipe her dreary ditty to the surge
All tumbling in the soft green !evel light,
He sits as quiet as a thick-mossed rock,

---

* Ogyges, the most ancient of Greek kings, reigned over Boetia in a time
of obscure antiquity. A son of Terra, the ancient earth deity, he married Thebe,
the daughter of Zeus. He was said to be of Egyptian origin.

K

And dreameth in his cold old savage way
Of gliding barges on the wine-dark waves,
And glowing shapes, and sweeter things than sleep,
But chiefly, while the restless twofold bat
Goes flapping round the rainy eaves above,
Where one broad opening letteth in the moon,
He starteth, thinking of that grey-haired man,
His sire: then oftentimes the white-armed child
Of thunder-bearing Jove, young Thebe, comes
And droops above him with her short sweet sighs
For Love distraught—for dear Love's faded sake
That weeps and sings and weeps itself to death
Because of casual eyes, and lips of frost,
And careless mutterings, and most weary years.

Bethink you, doth the wan Aegyptian count
This passion, wasting like an unfed flame,
Of any worth now; seeing that his thighs
Are shrunken to a span; and that the blood
Which used to spin tumultous down his sides
Of life in leaping moments of desire,
Is drying like a thin and sluggish stream
In withered channels—think you, doth he pause
For golden Thebe and her red young mouth?

Ah, golden Thebe—Thebe, weeping there,
Like some sweet wood-nymph wailing for a rock,
If Octis with the Apollonian face—
That fair-haired prophet of the sun and stars—
Could take a mist and dip it in the West
To clothe thy limbs of shine about with shine
And all the wonder of the amethyst,
He'd do it—kneeling like a slave for thee!
If he could find a dream to comfort thee,
He'd bring it: thinking little of his lore,
But marvelling greatly at those eyes of thine.
Yea, if the Shepherd waiting for thy steps,
Pent down amongst the dank black-weeded rims,
Could shed his life like rain about thy feet,
He'd count it sweetness past all sweets of love
To die by thee—his life's end in thy sight.

O but he loves the hunt, doth Ogyges!
And therefore should we blow the horn for him:
He, sitting mumbling in his surf-white cave
With helpless feet and alienated eyes,
Should hear the noises nathless dawn by dawn
Which send him wandering swiftly through the days
When like a springing cataract he leapt
From crag to crag, the strongest in the chase
To spear the lion, leopard, or the boar!
O but he loves the hunt; and, while the shouts
Of mighty winds are in this mountained World,
Behold the white bleak woodman, Winter, halts
And bends to him across a beard of snow
For wonder; seeing Summer in his looks
Because of dogs and calls from throats of hair
All in the savage hills of Hyria!
And, through the yellow evenings of the year,
What time September shows her mooned front
And poppies burnt to blackness droop for drouth,
The dear Demeter, splashed from heel to thigh
With spinning vine-blood, often stoops to him
To crush the grape against his wrinkled lips
Which sets him dreaming of the thickening wolves
In darkness, and the sound of moaning seas.
So with the blustering tempest doth he find
A stormy fellowship: for when the North
Comes reeling downwards with a breath like spears,
Where Dryope the lonely sits all night
And holds her sorrow crushed betwixt her palms,
He thinketh mostly of that time of times
When Zeus the Thunderer—broadly-blazing King—
Like some wild comet beautiful but fierce,
Leapt out of cloud and fire and smote the tops
Of black Ogygia with his red right hand,
At which great fragments tumbled to the Deeps—
The mighty fragments of a mountain-land—
And all the World became an awful Sea!

But, being tired, the hairless Ogyges
Best loveth night and dim forgetfulness!
"For", sayeth he, "to look for sleep is good
When every sleep is as a sleep of death
To men who live, yet know not why they live,

Nor how they live! I have no thought to tell
The people when this time of mine began;
But forest after forest grows and falls,
And rock by rock is wasted with the rime,
While I sit on and wait the end of all;
Here taking every footstep for a sign;
An ancient shadow whiter than the foam."

PYTHEAS*

Gaul, whose keel in far dim ages ploughed wan widths of polar sea—
Grey old sailor of Massilia, who hath woven wreath for thee?
Who amongst the world's high singers ever breathed the tale sublime
Of the man who coasted England in the misty dawn of Time?
Leaves of laurel, lights of music—these and these have never shed
Glory on the name unheard of—lustre on the vanished head!
Lords of Song, and these are many, never yet have raised the lay
For the white windbeaten seaman of a wild forgotten day!
Harp of shining son of Godhead still is as a voice august;
But the man who first saw Britain sleeps beneath unnoticed dust.

From the fair calm bays Hellenic—from the crescents and the bends
Round the walls of crystal Athens glowing in gold evening-ends—
Sailed abroad the grand strong father with his face towards the snow
Of the awful northern mountains, twenty centuries ago!
On the seas that none had heard of, by the shores where none had
    furled
Wing of canvas, passed this elder to the limits of the world!
Lurid limits loud with thunder and the roar of flaming cone—
Ghastly tracts of ice and whirlwind lying in a dim blind zone!
Bitter belts of naked region girt about by cliffs of fear
Where the Spirit of the Darkness dwells in heaven half the year!

Yea, against the wild weird Thule, steered the stranger through the
    gates
Opened by a fire eternal into tempest-trampled straits—
Thule lying like a nightmare on the borders of the Pole:
Neither land nor air nor water, but a mixture of the whole!
Dumb dead chaos, grey as spectre, now a mist and now a cloud,
Where the winds cry out for ever and the wave is always loud.
Here the lord of many waters, in the great exalted years,
Saw the sight that no man knows of—heard the sound that no man
    hears!
Felt that God was in the Shadow ere he turned his prow and sped
To the sweet green fields of England with the sunshine overhead.

---

* Pytheas, c. 360-290 B.C., famous as a geographer, astronomer, and philo-
sopher, also won fame by his travels. Starting from his native Massilia, the
modern Marseilles, he sailed round Britain and into the Baltic Sea.

In the day when pallid Persia fled before the Thracian steel,
By the land that now is London passed the strange Hellenic keel.
Up the bends of quiet river, hard by banks of grove and flower,
Sailed the father through a silence in the old majestic hour.
Not a sound of fin or feather, not a note of wave or breeze,
Vext the face of sleeping streamlets, broke the rest of stirless trees!
Not a foot was in the forest, not a voice was in the wood,
When the elder from Massilia over English waters stood!
All was new, and hushed, and holy—all was pure untrodden space
When the lord of many oceans turned to it a reverent face.

Man who knew resplendent Athens set and framed in silver sea,
Did not dream a dream of England—England of the years to be!
Friend of fathers like to Plato—bards august and hallowed seers—
Did not see that tenfold glory, Britain of the future years!
Spirit filled with Grecian music—songs that charm the dark away—
On that large supreme occasion, did not note diviner lay!
Did not hear the voice of Shakespeare—all the mighty life was still
Down the slopes that dipped to seaward, on the shoulders of the hill;
But the gold and green were brighter than the bloom of Thracian
    springs,
And a strange surpassing beauty shone upon the face of things.

In a grave that no man thinks of—back from far forgotten bays—
Sleeps the grey windbeaten sailor of the old exalted days.
He that coasted Wales and Dover—he that first saw Sussex plains,
Passed away with head unlaurelled in the wild Thessalian rains!
In a space by hand untended, by a fen of vapours blind,
Lies the king of many waters—out of sight and out of mind!
No one brings the yearly blossom—no one culls the flower of grace
For the shell of mighty father buried in that lonely place!
But the winds are low and holy, and the songs of sweetness flow
Where he fell asleep for ever, twenty centuries ago.

DAPHNE*

Daphne! Ladon's daughter, Daphne! Set thyself in silver light,
Take thy thoughts of fairest texture, weave them into words of
    white—
Weave the rhyme of rose-lipped Daphne, nymph of wooded stream
    and shade,
Flying love of bright Apollo,—fleeting type of faultless maid!
She, when followed from the forelands by the lord of lyre and lute,
Sped towards far-singing waters, past deep gardens flushed with fruit;
Took the path against Peneus, panted by its yellow banks;
Turned, and looked, and flew the faster through grey-tufted thicket
    ranks;
Flashed amongst high flowered sedges: leaped across the brook, and
    ran
Down to where the fourfold shadows of a nether glade began;
There she dropped, like falling Hesper, heavy hair of radiant head
Hiding all the young abundance of her beauty's white and red.

Came the yellow-tressed Far-darter—came the god whose feet are
    fire,
On his lips the name of Daphne, in his eyes a great desire;
Fond, full lips of lord and lover, sad because of suit denied;
Clear, grey eyes made keen by passion, panting, pained, unsatisfied.
Here he turned, and there he halted, now he paused, and now he
    flew,
Swifter than his sister's arrows, through soft dells of dreamy dew.
Vext with gleams of Ladon's daughter, dashed along the son of Jove,
Fast upon flower-trammelled Daphne fleeting on from grove to grove;
Flights of seawind hard behind him, breaths of bleak and whistling
    straits;
Drifts of driving cloud above him, like a troop of fierce-eyed fates!
So he reached the water-shallows; then he stayed his steps, and heard
Daphne drop upon the grasses, fluttering like a wounded bird.

---

* Daphne, daughter of the River Ladon and the goddess Terra, fled from
the passionate love of Apollo, and entreated the aid of the gods, who changed
her into a laurel-tree. Here the metamorphosis is effected fittingly by Pallas
Athene, the maiden goddess. Apollo thereafter crowned his head with the leaves
of the laurel, and made the tree sacred to his divinity.

Was there help for Ladon's daughter? Saturn's son is high and just:
Did he come between her beauty and the fierce Far-darter's lust?
As she lay, the helpless maiden, caught and bound in fast eclipse,
Did the lips of god drain pleasure from her sweet and swooning
    lips?
Now that these and all Love's treasures blushed, before the spoiler,
    bare,
Was the wrong that shall be nameless done, and seen, and suffered
    there?
No! for Zeus is King and Father. Weary nymph and fiery god,
Bend the knee alike before him—he is kind, and he is lord!
Therefore sing how clear-browed Pallas—Pallas, friend of prayerful
    maid,
Lifted dazzling Daphne lightly, bore her down the breathless glade,
Did the thing that Zeus commanded: so it came to pass that he
Who had chased a white-armed virgin, caught at her, and clasped a
    tree.

CAMPASPE*

Turn from the ways of this Woman! Campaspe we call her by name—
She is fairer than flowers of the fire—she is brighter than brightness
of flame.
As a song that strikes swift to the heart with the beat of the blood
of the South,
And a light and a leap and a smart, is the play of her perilous mouth.
Her eyes are as splendours that break in the rain at the set of the sun,
But turn from the steps of Campaspe—a Woman to look at and shun!

Dost thou know of the cunning of Beauty? take heed to thyself and
beware
Of the trap in the droop in the raiment—the snare in the folds of the
hair!
She is fulgent in flashes of pearl, the breeze with her breathing is
sweet,
But fly from the face of the girl—there is death in the fall of her
feet!
Is she maiden or marvel of marble? O rather a tigress at wait
To pounce on thy soul for her pastime—a leopard for love or for hate.

Woman of shadow and furnace! she biteth her lips to restrain
Speech that springs out when she sleepeth, by the stirs and the starts
of her pain.
As music half-shapen of sorrow, with its wants and its infinite wail,
Is the voice of Campaspe, the beauty at bay with her passion dead-
pale.
Go out from the courts of her loving, nor tempt the fierce dance of
desire
Where thy life would be shrivelled like stubble in the stress and the
fervour of fire!

I know of one, gentle as moonlight—she is sad as the shine of the
moon,
But touching the ways of her eyes are: she comes to my soul like a
tune—

* Campaspe was the beautiful mistress of King Alexander the Great, who
ordered Apelles to paint her. He fell in love with her, and was allowed by
Alexander to marry her. He reproduced her naked beauty in his famous picture
of Venus rising from the sea.

Like a tune that is filled with faint voices of the loved and the lost
 and the lone,
Doth this stranger abide with my silence: like a tune with a tremulous
 tone.
The leopard, we call her, Campaspe! I pluck at a rose and I stir
To think of this sweet-hearted maiden—what name is too tender for
 her?

DANTE AND VIRGIL

When lost Francesca sobbed her broken tale
 Of Love, and Sin, and boundless Agony;
While that wan Spirit by her side did wail
 And bite his lips for utter misery—
  The Grief which could not speak, nor hear, nor see;
So tender grew the superhuman face
Of one who listened, that a mighty trace
 Of superhuman Woe gave way, and pale,
The sudden light upstruggled to its place;
 While all his limbs began to faint and fail
With such excess of Pity! But, behind,
 The Roman Virgil stood—the calm, the wise—
 With not a shadow in his regal eyes,
A stately type of all his stately kind!

TO DAMASCUS

Where the sinister sun of the Syrians beat
    On the brittle bright stubble,
And the camels fell back from the swords of the heat,
Came Saul with a fire in the soles of his feet,
    And a forehead of trouble.

And terrified faces to left and to right,
    Before and behind him,
Fled away with the speed of a maddening fright,
To the cloughs of the bat, and the chasms of night,
Each hoping the zealot would fail in his flight
    To find him and bind him.

For, behold you, the strong man of Tarsus came down
    With breathings of slaughter,
From the priests of the city, the chiefs of the town,
(The lords with the sword, and the sires with the gown),
To harry the Christians, and trample, and drown,
    And waste them like water.

He was *ever* a fighter, this son of the Jews—
    A fighter in earnest;
And the Lord took delight in the strength of his thews,
For He knew he was one of the few He could choose
To fight out His battles, and carry His news
Of a marvellous Truth through the dark, and the dews,
    And the desert-lands furnaced!

He knew he was one of the few He could take
    For His Mission Supernal;
Whose feet would not falter, whose limbs would not ache,
Through the waterless lands of the thorn and the snake,
And the ways of the wild—bearing up for the sake
    Of a Beauty eternal.

And therefore the road to Damascus was burned
    With a swift, sudden brightness;
While Saul, with his face in the bitter dust, learned
Of the sin which he did, ere he tumbled, and turned
    Aghast at God's whiteness!

Of the sin which he did, ere he covered his head
    From the strange revelation.
But, thereafter, you know of the life that he led;
How he preached to the peoples, and suffered, and sped
With the wonderful words which his Master had said,
    From nation to nation.

Now would we be like him, who suffer and see,
    If the Chooser should choose us!
For I tell you, brave brothers, whoever you be,
It is right, till all learn to look further, and see,
    That our Master should use us!

It is right, till all learn to discover and class,
    That our Master should task us:
For now we may judge of the Truth through a glass;
And the road over which they must evermore pass,
Who would think for the many, and fight for the mass,
    Is the road to Damascus.

KING SAUL AT GILBOA

With noise of battle and the dust of fray,
Half-hid in fog, the gloomy mountain lay;
But Succoth's watchers from their outer fields
Saw fits of flame and gleams of clashing shields
For where the yellow river draws its spring
The hosts of Israel travelled thundering!
There, beating like the storm that sweeps to sea
Across the reefs of chafing Galilee,
The car of Abner and the sword of Saul
Drave Gaza down Gilboa's southern wall;
But swift and sure the spears of Ekron flew,
Till peak and slope were drenched with bloody dew!
"Shout, Timnath, shout!" the blazing leaders cried,
And hurled the stone, and dashed the stave aside:
"Shout, Timnath, shout! Let Hazor hold the height,
Bend the long bow and break the lords of fight!"
From every hand the swarthy strangers sprang,
Chief leaped on chief, with buckler buckler rang!
The flower of armies! set in Syrian heat,
The ridges clamoured under labouring feet;
Nor stayed the warriors till from Salim's road
The crescent horns of Abner's squadrons glowed.
Then, like a shooting splendour on the wing,
The strong-armed son of Kish came thundering;
And as in Autumn's fall, when woods are bare,
Two adverse tempests meet in middle air,
So Saul and Achish, grim with heat and hate,
Met by the brooks and shook the scales of Fate;
For now the struggle swayed, and, firm as rocks
Against the storm-wind of the equinox,
The rallied lords of Judah stood and bore
All day the fiery tides of fourfold war.

But he that fasted in the secret cave,
And called up Samuel from the quiet grave,
And stood with darkness and the mantled ghosts
A bitter night on shrill Samarian coasts,
Knew well the end: of how the futile sword

Of Israel would be broken by the Lord;
How Gath would triumph with the tawny line
That bend the knee at Dagon's brittle shrine;
And how the race of Kish would fall to wreck
Because of vengeance stayed at Amalek;
Yet strove the sunlike king, nor rested hand
Till yellow evening filled the level land;
Then Judah reeled before a biting hail
Of sudden arrows shot from Akor's vale,
Where Libnah, lapped in blood from thigh to heel,
Drew the tense string and pierced the quivering steel.
There fell the sons of Saul, and, man by man,
The chiefs of Israel up to Jonathan;
And, while swift Achish stooped and caught the spoil,
Ten chosen archers red with sanguine toil
Sped after Saul, who, faint and sick and sore
With many wounds, had left the thick of war:
He, like a baffled bull by hunters prest,
Turned sharp about and faced the flooded west,
And saw the star-like spears and moony spokes
Gleam from the rocks and lighten through the oaks;
A sea of splendour! How the chariots rolled
On wheels of blinding brightness manifold!
While stumbling over spike and spine and spur
Of sultry lands, escaped the son of Ner
With smitten men! At this the front of Saul
Grew darker than a blasted tower wall;
And seeing how there crouched upon his right
Aghast with fear a black Amalekite,
He called and said, "I pray thee, man of pain,
Red from the scourge, and recent from the chain,
Set thou thy face to mine and stoutly stand
With yonder bloody sword-hilt in thine hand
And fall upon me." But the faltering hind
Stood trembling like a willow in the wind.
Then further, Saul: "Lest Ashdod's vaunting hosts
Should bear me captive to their bleak-blown coasts,
I pray thee, smite me: seeing peace has fled,
And rest lies wholly with the quiet dead."
At this a flood of sunset broke, and smote
Keen blazing sapphires round a kingly throat,
Touched arm and shoulder, glittered in the crest,
And made swift starlights on a jewelled breast!

So, starting forward like a loosened hound,
The stranger clutched the sword and wheeled it round,
And struck the Lord's Anointed! Fierce and fleet,
Philistia came with shouts and clattering feet;
By gaping gorges and by rough defile,
Dark Ashdod beat across a dusty mile;
Hot Hazor's bowmen toiled from spire to spire;
And Gath sprang upwards like a gust of fire!
On either side did Libnah's lords appear;
And brass-clad Timnath thundered in the rear!
"Mark, Achish, mark!"—South-west and south there sped
A dabbled hireling from the dreadful dead!
"Mark, Achish, mark!"—The mighty front of Saul,
Great in his life and god-like in his fall!
This was the arm that broke Philistia's pride
Where Kishon chafes his seaward-going tide!
This was the sword that smote till set of sun
Red Gath from Micmash unto Ajalon!
Low in the dust. And Israel scattered far!
And dead the trumps, and crushed the hoofs of war!
So fell the king! as it was said by him
Who hid his forehead in a mantle dim
At bleak Endor, what time unholy rites
Vext the long sleep of still Samarian heights:
For bowed to earth before the hoary Priest
Did he of Kish withstand the smoking feast,
To fast, in darkness and in sackcloth rolled,
And house with wild things in the biting cold;
Because of sharpness lent to Gaza's sword,
And Judah widowed by the angry Lord.

So Silence came! As when the outer verge
Of Carmel takes the white and whistling surge,
Hoarse hollow noises fill the caves and roar
Along the margins of the echoing shore,
Thus War had thundered! But as Evening breaks
Across the silver of Assyrian lakes,
When reapers rest, and through the level red
Of sunset, peace like holy oil is shed,
Thus Silence fell; but Israel's daughters crept
Outside their thresholds, waited, watched, and wept.

Then they that dwell beyond the flats and fens
Of sullen Jordon, and in gelid glens
Of Jabesh-Gilead, chosen chiefs and few,
Around their loins the hasty girdle drew,
And faced the forests huddled fold on fold,
And dells of glimmering greenness manifold,
What time Orion in the west did set
A shining foot on hills of wind and wet:
These journeyed nightly till they reached the capes
Where Ashdod revelled over heated grapes;
And, while the feast was loud and scouts were turned,
From Saul's bound body cord by cord they burned,
And bore the king athwart the place of tombs,
And hasted eastward through the tufted glooms;
Nor broke the cake, nor stayed the step till Morn
Shot over Debir's cones and crags forlorn!

From Jabesh then the weeping virgins came;
In Jabesh then they built the funeral flame;
With costly woods they piled the lordly pyre,
Brought yellow oils and fed the perfect fire;
While round the crescent stately Elders spread
The flashing armour of the mighty dead,
With crown and spear, and all the trophies won
From many wars by Israel's dreadful Son.
Thence, when the feet of Evening paused and stood
On shadowy mountains and the roaring flood
(As through a rushing twilight full of rain
The weak Moon looked athwart Gadar's plain),
The younger warriors bore the urn, and broke
The humid turf about a wintering oak,
And buried Saul; and, fasting, went their ways,
And hid their faces seven nights and days.

CAMPED BY THE CREEK

JIM THE SPLITTER

The bard who is singing of Wollombi Jim
Is hardly just now in the requisite trim
    To sit on his Pegasus fairly;
Besides, he is bluntly informed by the Muse
That Jim is a subject no singer should choose;
    For Jim is poetical rarely.

But being full up of the myths that are Greek—
Of the classic and "noble and nude and antique",
    Which means, not a rag but the pelt on,
This poet intends to give Daphne the slip,
For the sake of a hero in moleskin and kip
    With a jumper and snake-buckle belt on.

No party is Jim of the Pericles type:
He is modern right up from the toe to the pipe;
    And, being no reader or roamer,
He hasn't Euripides much in the head;
And, let it be carefully, tenderly said,
    He never has analysed Homer.

He can roar out a song of the twopenny-kind;
But, knowing the beggar so well, I'm inclined
    To believe that a "par" about Kelly,
The rascal who skulked under shadow of curse,
Is more in his line than the happiest verse
    On the glittering pages of Shelley.

You musn't, however, adjudge him in haste,
Because a red robber is more to his taste
    Than Ruskin, Rossetti, or Dante!
You see he was bred in a bangalow wood
And bangalow pith was the principal food
    His mother served out in her shanty.

His knowledge is this—he can tell in the dark
What timber will split, by the feel of the bark;
    And, rough as his manner of speech is,

His wits to the fore he can readily bring
In passing off ash as the genuine thing,
     When scarce in the forest the beech is.

In "girthing" a tree that he sells "in the round",
He assumes as a rule that its body is sound,
     And measures—*forgetting to bark it!*
He may be a ninny; but still the old dog
Can plug to perfection the pipe of a log
     And "palm it" away on the market.

He splits a fair shingle; but holds to the rule
Of his father's, and haply his grandfather's, school—
     Which means that he never has blundered,
When tying his shingles, by slinging in more
Than the recognized number of ninety and four,
     To the bundle he sells for a hundred!

When asked by the market for ironbark red,
It always occurs to the Wollombi head
     To do a "mahogany" swindle.
In forests where never the ironbark grew,
When Jim is at work, it would flabbergast you
     To see how the "ironbarks" dwindle!

He can stick to the saddle can Wollombi Jim;
And when a buckjumper dispenses with him
     The leather goes off with the rider.
And, as to a team, over gully and hill
He can travel with twelve on the breadth of a quill,
     And boss the unlucky "offsider".

He shines at his best at the tiller of saw,
On the top of the pit, where his whisper is law
     To the gentlemen working below him.
When the pair of them pause in a circle of dust,
Like a monarch he *poses* exalted, august—
     There's nothing this planet can show him!

For a man is a *man* who can "sharpen" and "set";
And *he* is the only thing masculine yet,
     According to sawyer and splitter;

Or rather according to Wollombi Jim!
And nothing will tempt me to differ with him,
    For Jim is a bit of a hitter.

But, being full up, we'll allow him to rip,
Along with his lingo, his saw, and his whip—
    He isn't the classical "notion";
And, after a night in his "humpy", you see,
A person of orthodox habits would be
    Refreshed by a dip in the ocean.

To tot him right up from the heel to the head,
He isn't the Grecian of whom we have read:
    His face is a trifle too shady.
The nymph in green valleys of Thessaly dim
Would never "jack up" her old lover for him,
    For *she* has the tastes of a lady.

So much for our hero! A statuesque foot
Would suffer by wearing that heavy-nailed boot:
    Its owner is hardly Achilles!
However, he's happy. He cuts a great "fig"—
In the land where a coat is no part of the "rig"—
    In the country of damper and "billies".

CAMPED BY THE CREEK

"All day a strong sun has been drinking
   The ponds in the Wattletree Glen;
And now as they're puddles, I'm thinking
   We were wise to head hitherwards, men!
The country is heavy to nor'ard,
   But Lord, how you rattled along!
Jack's chestnut's best leg was put for'ard,
   And the bay from the start galloped strong;
But for bottom, I'd stake my existence,
   There's none of the lot like the mare;
For look! she has come the whole distance
   With never the 'turn of a hair'.

"But now let us stop, for the 'super'
   Will want us tomorrow by noon;
And as he can swear like a trooper,
   We can't be a minute too soon.
Here, Dick, you can hobble the filly
   And chestnut, but don't take a week;
And, Jack, hurry off with the billy
   And fill it. We'll camp by the creek."

So spoke the old stockman, and quickly
   We made ourselves snug for the night;
The smoke-wreaths above us curled thickly,
   For our pipes were the first thing alight!
As we sat round a fire that only
   A well-seasoned Bushman can make,
Far forests grew silent and lonely,
   Though the paw was astir in the brake.
But not till our supper was ended,
   And not till old Bill was asleep,
Did wild things by wonder attended
   In shot of our camping-ground creep.
Scared eyes from thick tuft and tree-hollow
   Gleamed out thro' the forest-boles stark;
And ever a hurry would follow
   Of fugitive feet in the dark.

While Dick and I yarned and talked over
　　Old times that had gone like the sun,
The wail of the desolate plover
　　Came up from the swamps in the run.
And sniffing our supper, elated,
　　From his den the red dingo crawled out;
But skulked in the darkness, and waited,
　　Like a cunning but cowardly scout.
Thereafter came sleep that soon falls on
　　A man who has ridden all day;
And when midnight had deepened the palls on
　　The hills, we were snoring away.
But ere we dozed off, the wild noises
　　Of forest, of fen, and of stream,
Grew strange, and were one with the voices
　　That died with a sweet semi-dream.
And the tones of the waterfall, blended
　　With the song of the wind on the shore,
Became a soft psalm that ascended,
　　Grew far, and we heard it no more.

THE BARCOO

(The Squatters' Song)

I

From the runs of the Narran, wide-dotted with sheep,
    And loud with the lowing of cattle,
We speed for a Land where the strange Forests sleep
    And the hidden creeks bubble and brattle!
Now call on the horses, and leave the blind courses
    And sources of rivers that all of us know;
For, crossing the ridges, and passing the ledges,
And running up gorges, we'll come to the verges
    Of gullies where waters eternally flow!
Oh! the herds they will rush down the spurs of the hill
    To feed on the grasses so cool and so sweet;
And I think that my life with delight will stand still
    When we halt with the pleasant Barcoo at our feet.

II

Good-bye to the Barwan and brigalow scrubs!
    Adieu to the Culgoä ranges!
But look for the mulga and salt-bitten shrubs,
    Though the face of the forest-land changes.
The leagues we may travel down beds of hot gravel,
    And clay-crusted reaches where moisture hath been,
While searching for waters, may vex us and thwart us,
Yet who would be quailing, or fainting, or failing?
    Not you, who are men of the Narran, I ween!
When we leave the dry channels away to the South,
    And reach the far plains we are journeying to,
We will cry, though our lips may be glued with the drouth,
    "Hip, hip, and hurrah for the pleasant Barcoo!"

SONG OF THE CATTLE-HUNTERS

While the morning light beams on the fern-matted streams,
    And the water-pools flash in its glow,
Down the ridges we fly, with a loud ringing cry—
    Down the ridges and gullies we go!
And the cattle we hunt, they are racing in front,
    With a roar like the thunder of waves;
As the beat and the beat of our swift horses' feet
    Start the echoes away from their caves!
        As the beat and the beat
        Of our swift horses' feet
    Start the echoes away from their caves!

Like a wintery shore that the waters ride o'er,
    All the lowlands are filling with sound;
For swiftly we gain where the herds on the plain,
    Like a tempest, are tearing the ground!
And we'll follow them hard to the rails of the yard,
    Over gulches and mountain-tops grey,
Where the beat and the beat of our swift horses' feet
    Will die with the echoes away!
        Where the beat and the beat
        Of our swift horses' feet
    Will die with the echoes away!

KINGSBOROUGH*

A waving of hats and of hands,
    The voices of thousands in one,
A shout from the Ring and the Stands,
    And a glitter of heads in the sun!
"They are off—they are off", is the roar,
    As the cracks settle down to the race,
With the "yellow and black" to the fore,
    And the Panic blood forcing the pace.

At the back of the course, and away
    Where the running ground home again wheels,
Grubb travels in front on the "bay"
    With a feather-weight hard at his heels.
But Yeomans, you see, is "about",
    And the wily New Zealander waits,
Though the high-blooded flyer is out
    Whose rider and colours are Tait's.

Look! Ashworth comes on with a run
    To the head of the Levity colt;
And the fleet—the magnificent son
    Of Panic is "shooting his bolt".
Hurrah for the Weatherbit strain!
    A Fireworks is first in the straight;
And *"a Kelpie will win it again"*,
    Is the roar from the ring to the gate.

The leader must have it—but no!
    For see, full of running, behind
A beautiful wonderful foe
    With the speed of the thunder and wind!
A flashing of whips, and a cry,
    And Ashworth "sits down" on his horse
With Kingsborough's head at his thigh,
    And the "field" scattered over the course!

---

* The race for the Melbourne Stakes, 1875.—H.K.
Kingsborough was owned by Sir Hercules Robinson, Governor of New
South Wales, 1872-9, ridden by Yeomans, carried two stone weight, and won
in 3 minutes 18 seconds—a record time for the race.—Ed.

In a clamour of calls and acclaim,
    The pair race away from the "ruck":
The horse to the last of it game—
    A marvel of muscle and pluck!
But the foot of the Sappho is there,
    And Kingston's invincible strength;
And the numbers go up in the air—
    The colt is the first by a length!

The first and the favourite too!
    The terror that came from his stall,
With the spirit of fire and of dew,
    To show the road home to them all!
From the back of the field to the straight,
    He has "come", as is ever his wont,
And carried his welter-like weight,
    Like a tradesman, right through to the front.

Nor wonder at cheering a whit,
    For this is the popular horse
That never was beaten when "fit"
    By any four hoofs on the course!
To starter for Leger or Cup
    Has he ever shown feather of fear
When saddle and rider were up
    And the case to be argued was clear?

No! rather the questionless pluck
    Of the blood unaccustomed to yield
Preferred to "spread-eagle" the ruck,
    And make a long tail of the "field".
Bear witness, ye lovers of sport,
    To races of which he can boast,
When flyer by flyer was caught
    And beaten by lengths on the post!

Lo! this is the beautiful bay—
    Of many, the marvellous one
Who showed us last season the way
    That a Leger should always be won.
There was something to look at and learn,
    Ye shrewd irreproachable "touts",
When the Panic colt tired at the turn,
    And the thing was all over—but shouts!

Ay, that was the "spin" when the twain
    Came locked by the bend of the course,
The Zetlander pulling his rein,
    And the veteran hard on his horse!
When Ashworth was "riding" 'twas late
    For his friends to applaud on the Stands
And the Sappho colt entered the straight
    With the race of the year in his hands.

Just look at his withers—his thighs!
    And the way that he carries his head!
Has Richmond more wonderful eyes,
    Or Melbourne that spring in his tread?
The grand—the intelligent glance
    From a spirit that fathoms and feels
Makes the heart of a horse-lover dance
    Till the warmblooded life in him reels.

What care have I ever to know
    His owner by sight or by name!
The horse that I glory in so
    Is still the magnificent same!
I own I am proud of the pluck
    Of the sportsman that never was bought;
But the nag that "spread-eagled the ruck"
    Is bound to be first in my thought.

For who that has masculine flame,
    Or who that is thorough at all,
Can help feeling joy in the fame
    Of this king of the kings of the stall?
What odds if assumption has sealed
    His soulless hereafter abode,
So long as he shows to his "field"
    The gleam of his hoofs, and the road.

THE WARRIGAL*

Through forest boles the stormwind rolls,
    Vext of the sea-driven rain,
And up in the clift, through many a rift,
    The voices of torrents complain.
The sad marsh-fowl and the lonely owl
    Are heard in the fog-wreaths grey,
When the Warrigal wakes, and listens, and takes
    To the woods that shelter the prey.

In the gully-deeps, the blind creek sleeps;
    And the silver, showery, moon
Glides over the hills, and floats, and fills,
    And dreams in the dark lagoon;
While halting hard by the station yard,
    Aghast at the hut-flame nigh,
The Warrigal yells, and the flats and fells
    Are loud with his dismal cry.

On the topmost peak of mountains bleak,
    The south wind sobs, and strays
Through moaning pine, and turpentine,
    And the rippling runnel ways;
And strong streams flow, and great mists go,
    Where the Warrigal starts to hear
The watch-dog's bark break sharp in the dark,
    And flees like a phantom of Fear!

The swift rains beat, and the thunders fleet
    On the wings of the fiery gale,
And down in the glen of pool and fen,
    The wild gums whistle and wail,
As over the plains, and past the chains
    Of waterholes glimmering deep,
The Warrigal flies from the Shepherd's cries,
    And the clamour of dogs and sheep.

---

* The Dingo, or Wild Dog of Australia.—H.K.

The Warrigal's lair is pent in bare
    Black rocks at the gorge's mouth:
It is set in ways where Summer strays
    With the sprites of flame and drouth;
But when the heights are touched with lights
    Of hoarfrost, sleet, and shine,
His bed is made of the dead grass-blade
    And the leaves of the windy pine.

He roves through the lands of sultry sands,
    He hunts in the iron range,
Untamed as surge of the far sea verge,
    And fierce and fickle and strange.
The white man's track and the haunts of the black
    He shuns, and shudders to see;
For his joy he tastes in lonely wastes
    Where his mates are torrent and tree.

BILL THE BULLOCK DRIVER

The leaders of millions—the lords of the lands
    Who sway the wide world with their will,
And shake the great globe with the strength of their hands,
    Flash past us—unnoticed by Bill.

The elders of Science who measure the spheres,
    And weigh the vast bulk of the sun—
Who see the grand lights beyond aeons of years,
    Are less than a bullock to *one*.

The singers that sweeten all time with their song—
    Pure voices that make us forget
Humanity's drama of marvellous wrong,
    To Bill are as mysteries yet.

By thunders of battle and nations uphurled,
    Bill's sympathies never were stirred:
The helmsmen who stand at the wheel of the world
    By him are unknown and unheard.

What trouble has Bill for the ruin of lands,
    Or the quarrels of temple and throne,
So long as the whip that he holds in his hands,
    And the team that he drives, are his own?

As straight and as sound as a slab without crack,
    Our Bill is a king in his way:
Though he camps by the side of a shingle track,
    And sleeps on the bed of his dray.

A whiplash to him is as dear as a rose
    Would be to a delicate maid:
He carried his darlings wherever he goes
    In a pocket-book tattered and frayed.

The joy of a bard when he happens to write
    A song like the song of his dream
Is nothing at all to our hero's delight
    In the pluck and the strength of his team.

For the kings of the earth—for the faces august
    Of princes, the millions may shout:
To Bill as he lumbers along in the dust,
    A bullock's the grandest thing out.

His fourfooted friends are the friends of his choice—
    No lover is Bill of your dames;
But the cattle that turn at the sound of his voice
    Have the sweetest of features and names.

A father's chief joy is a favourite son
    When he reaches some eminent goal;
But the pride of Bill's heart is the hairy-legged one
    That pulls with a will at the pole.

His dray is no living, responsible thing,
    But he gives it the gender of life;
And, seeing his fancy is free in the wing,
    It suits him as well as a wife.

He thrives like an Arab. Between the two wheels
    Is his bedroom, where, lying up-curled,
He thinks for himself like a sultan, and feels
    That his home is the best in the world.

For, even though cattle like subjects will break
    At times from the yoke and the band,
Bill knows how to act when his rule is at stake,
    And is therefore a lord of the land.

Of course he must dream; but be sure that his dreams,
    If happy, must compass—alas!—
Fat bullocks at feed by improbable streams,
    Knee-deep in improbable grass.

No poet is Bill; for the visions of night
    To him are as visions of day;
And the pipe that in sleep he endeavours to light
    Is the pipe that he smokes on the dray.

To the mighty, magnificent temples of God
    In the hearts of the dominant hills
Bill's eyes are as blind as the fire-blackened clod
    That burns far away from the rills.

Through beautiful, bountiful forests that screen
    A marvel of blossoms from heat—
Whose lights are the mellow and golden, and green—
    Bill walks with irreverent feet.

The manifold splendours of mountain and wood
    By Bill like nonentities slip:
He loves the black myrtle because it is good
    As a handle to lash to his whip.

And thus through the world, with a swing in his tread,
    Our hero self-satisfied goes;
With his cabbage-tree hat on the back of his head,
    And the string of it under his nose.

Poor Bullocky Bill! In the circles select
    Of the scholars he hasn't a place;
But he walks like a *man* with his forehead erect,
    And he looks at God's day in the face.

For, rough as he seems, he would shudder to wrong
    A dog with the loss of a hair;
And the angels of shine and superlative song
    See his heart and the deity there.

Few know him indeed; but the beauty that glows
    In the forest is loveliness still;
And Providence helping the life of the rose
    Is a Friend and a Father to Bill.

M

SONG OF THE SHINGLE-SPLITTERS

In dark wild woods, where the lone owl broods
    And the dingoes nightly yell—
Where the curlew's cry goes floating by,
    We splitters of shingles dwell.
And all day through, from the time of the dew
    To the hour when the mopoke calls,
Our mallets ring where the woodbirds sing
    Sweet hymns by the waterfalls.
And all night long we are lulled by the song
    Of gales in the grand old trees;
And in the breaks we can hear the lakes
    And the moan of the distant seas.
        For afar from heat and dust of street,
           And hall and turret, and dome,
        In forest deep, where the torrents leap,
           Is the shingle-splitter's home.

The dweller in town may lie upon down,
    And own his palace and park:
We envy him not his prosperous lot,
    Though we slumber on sheets of bark.
Our food is rough, but we have enough;
    Our drink is better than wine:
For cool creeks flow wherever we go,
    Shut in from the hot sunshine.
Though rude our roof, it is weather-proof,
    And at the end of the days
We sit and smoke over yarn and joke,
    By the bush-fire's sturdy blaze.
        For away from din, and sorrow and sin,
           Where troubles but rarely come,
        We jog along, like a merry song,
           In the shingle-splitter's home.

What though our work be heavy, we shirk
    From nothing beneath the sun;
And toil is sweet to those who can eat
    And rest when the day is done.
In the Sabbath-time we hear no chime,

No sound of the Sunday bells;
But yet Heaven smiles on the forest aisles,
And God in the woodland dwells.
We listen to notes from the million throats
Of chorister birds on high,
Our psalm is the breeze in the lordly trees,
And our dome is the broad blue sky.
Oh! a brave, frank life, unsmitten by strife,
We live wherever we roam,
And our hearts are free as the great strong sea,
In the shingle-splitter's home.

BILLY VICKERS

No song is this of leaf and bird
        And gracious waters flowing—
I'm sick at heart, for I have heard
        Big Billy Vickers "blowing".

He'd never take a leading place
        In chambers legislative:
This booby with the vacant face—
        This hoddy-doddy native!

Indeed, I'm forced to say aside
        To you, O reader, solely,
He only wants the horns and hide
        To be a bullock wholly.

But, like all noodles, he is vain;
        And, when his tongue is wagging,
I feel inclined to copy Cain,
        And drop him for his bragging.

He, being bush bred, stands of course
        Six feet his dirty socks in.
His lingo is confined to horse,
        And plough, and pig, and oxen.

Two years ago, he'd less to say
        Within his little circuit;
But now he has, besides a dray
        A team of twelve to work it.

No wonder is it that he feels
        Inclined to clack and rattle
About his bullocks and his wheels—
        He owns a dozen cattle.

In short, to be exact and blunt,
    In his own estimation
He's "out-and-out" the head and front
    Top-sawyer of creation!

For, mark me, he can "sit a buck"
    For hours and hours together;
And never horse has had the luck
    To pitch him from the leather.

If ever he should have a "spill"
    Upon the grass or gravel,
Be sure of this, the saddle will
    With Billy Vickers travel.

At punching oxen, you may guess
    There's nothing out can "camp" him:
He has, in fact, the slouch and dress
    Which bullock-driver stamp him.

I do not mean to give offence,
    But I have vainly striven
To ferret out the difference
    'Twixt driver and the driven.

Of course, the statements herein made
    In every other stanza
Are Billy's own; and I'm afraid
    They're stark extravaganza.

I feel constrained to treat as trash
    His noisy fiddle-faddle
About his doings with the lash—
    His feats upon the saddle.

But grant he "knows his way about",
    Or grant that he is silly,
There cannot be the slightest doubt
    Of Billy's faith in Billy.

Of all the doings of the day
　　His ignorance is utter;
But he can quote the price of hay—
　　The current rate of butter.

His notions of our leading men
　　Are mixed and misty very:
He knows a Cochin-China hen—
　　He never speaks of Berry.

As you'll assume, he hasn't heard
　　Of Madame Patti's singing;
But, I will stake my solemn word,
　　He knows what maize is bringing.

Surrounded by majestic peaks—
　　By lordly mountain ranges,
Where highest voice of thunder speaks—
　　His aspect never changes.

The grand Pacific there beyond
　　His dirty hut is glowing:
He only sees a big salt pond,
　　O'er which his grain is going.

The sea that covers half the sphere,
　　With all its stately speeches,
Is held by Bill to be a mere
　　Broad highway for his peaches.

Through Nature's splendid temples he
　　Plods, under mountains hoary;
But he has not the eyes to see
　　Their grandeur and their glory.

A bullock in a biped's boot,
　　I iterate, is Billy!
He crushes with a careless foot
　　The touching water-lily.

I've said enough—I'll let him go!
    If he could read these verses,
He'd pepper me for hours, I know,
    With his peculiar curses.

But this is sure, he'll never change
    His manners loud and "flashy";
Nor learn with neatness to arrange
    His clothing cheap and trashy.

Like other louts, he'll jog along,
    And swig at shanty liquors,
And chew and spit. Here ends the song
    Of Mr Billy Vickers.

THE IRISHMAN'S PIG

THE SONG OF NINIAN MELVILLE*

Sing the song of noisy Ninny—hang the Muses—spit it out!
(Tuneful Nine, ye needn't help me—poet knows his way about!)
Sling me here a penny whistle—look alive, and let me slip
Into Ninny like a father—Ninny with the nimble lip.
Mister Melville, straight descendant from Professor Huxley's ape,
Started life as mute for daddy—pulling faces, sporting crape;
But, alas, he didn't like it—lots of work and little pay!
Nature whispered, "You're a windbag—play your cards another way."

Mister Melville picked the hint up—pitched the coffin "biz" to pot:
Paid his bills, or didn't pay them—doesn't matter now a jot!—
Twigging how the bread was buttered, he commenced a "waiting
    game";
Pulled the strings upon the quiet—no one "tumbled" to his aim.
Paine, he purchased, Strauss, he borrowed—read a page or two of
    each:
Posed before his father's porkers—made to them his maiden speech.
Then he spluttered, "*Ninny has it!* Nin will keep himself in clothes,
Like that gutter Tully, Bradlaugh, leading noodles by the nose!"

In the fly-blown village pothouse, where a dribbling bag of beer
Passes for a human being, Nin commenced his new career—
Talked about the "Christian swindle"—cut the Bible into bits—
Shook his fist at Mark and Matthew—gave the twelve Apostles fits:
Slipped into the priests and parsons—hammered at the British
    Court—
Boozy boobies were astonished: lubbers of the Lambton sort!
Yards of ear were cocked to listen—yards of mouth began to shout,
"*Here's a cove as is long-headed—Ninny knows his way about!*"

Mister Melville was delighted—game in hand was paying well:
Fools and coin don't hang together—Nin became a howling swell!
Took to "stumping" on the Racecourse—cut the old debating club:
Wouldn't do for mighty Ninny now to mount a local tub!

---

* Ninian Melville, born in Sydney in 1843, was a cabinet-maker who became
Alderman and Mayor of Newtown, M.L.A. for Northumberland from 1880 to
1894, and from 1889 to 1894 Chairman of Committees and Deputy Speaker
in the New South Wales Parliament, thus occupying the chair which he had
made in 1886 as cabinet-maker.

Thornton's Column was his platform: here our orator began
Hitting at the yellow heathen—cracking up the "working man"—
Spitting out at Immigration: roaring, like a worried bull,
At the lucre made on tallow—at the profit raised on wool!

Said our Ninny to our Ninny, "I have not the slightest doubt
Soaping down the ''orny-'anded' is the safest 'bizness' out!
Little work for spanking wages—this is just the thing they like,
So I'll prop the eight hours swindle—be the boss in every strike.
In the end, I'll pull a pot off—what I'm at is bound to take:
Ninny sees a bit before him—Ninny's eyes are wide-awake!
When the boobies make me member, Parkes, of course, will offer tip—
I will take the first fat billet—then my frouzy friends may rip!"

So it came to pass that Melville—*Mister* Melville, I should say—
Dodged about with deputations, half a dozen times a day!
Started strikes and bossed the strikers—damned employers, every one,
On the Column—off the Column—in the shanty—in the sun!
"Down with masters—up with wages! keep the 'pigtail' out of this!"
This is what our Ninny shouted—game, you see, of hit or miss!
World, of course, is full of noodles—some who bray at Wallsend sent
Thing we know to be a windbag bounding into Parliament!

Common story, this of Ninny! many fellows of his breed
Prowl about to bone the guinea, up to dirty tricks indeed!
Haven't now the time to tan them; but, by Jove, I'd like to tan
Back of that immense imposter that they call the "working man"!
Drag upon our just employers—sponger on a worn-out wife—
Boozing in some alley pothouse every evening of his life!
Type he is of Nin's supporters: tot him up and tot him down,
He would back old Nick tomorrow for the sake of half a 'crown!

House with high, august traditions—Chamber where the voice of
    Lowe,
And the lordly words of Wentworth sounded thirty years ago—
Halls familiar to our fathers, where, in days exalted, rang
All the tones of all the feeling which ennobled Bland and Lang—
We in ashes—we in sackcloth, sorrow for the insult cast
By a crowd of bitter boobies on the grandeur of your past!
Take again your penny whistle—boy, it is no good to me:
Last invention is a bladder with the title of M.P.!

THE SAWYER WHO WORKS
ON THE TOP *
(Dedicated to the Premier)

Capacious of nostril and cheek,
    Gigantic in limb and in paw,
Behold him—the "growth of a week"—
    A-working the Government Saw!
What manner of labour is his
    Who comes from a "Brummagen" shop
With "charlatan" stamped on his phiz—
    The Sawyer who works on the top?

We ask—are his doings a bit
    Like what you expect him to do?
Did you set him there over the pit
    To saw all your liberty through?
Is Freedom the timbers to tear?
    Ye simpletons, when will ye stop
His heaving and cleaving unfair—
    The Sawyer who works on the top?

Is he fit for his eminent post?
    Does he know how to "sharpen" and "set"?
In spite of his swagger—his boast,
    You know he is Brummagen yet!
The skill that can "cut by the chalk"
    Has never been under his mop—
He is only a barrel of talk,
    The Sawyer who works on the top.

---

* This attack on Henry Parkes, then Premier of New South Wales (1879), makes use of the fact that Parkes was a bone and ivory turner in Birmingham and had his own business there to condemn him as only "Brummagen"— cheap goods of inferior quality from Birmingham. Like "The Gagging Bill", the satire was provoked by Kendall's anger at the infringement of freedom of speech he saw in the Parliamentary Powers and Privileges Bill which Parkes supported.

Some trees that he wishes to rend
    Are green in their fastnesses yet:
Then shelter them on to the end—
    These forests by Liberty set.
The beautiful growths that ye love
    He is seeking to level and top;
Then down from his prominence shove
    The Sawyer who works on the top.

Start out and select, as ye can,
    From yonder promiscuous lot
Some straight-away thorough-bred man,
    Who knows what to "cut" and what not!
Just give him control of the tools,
    And down from his pedestal drop
This doll of old women and fools—
    The Sawyer who works on the top.

THE "IRISHMAN'S PIG" *

A "funny" man down in the land of the South,
With a pen in his paw and a grin on his mouth,
Went sailing along in a Methodist boat;

---

* This satire was published on 21st August 1880 in the *Freeman's Journal*, the organ of Roman Catholic opinion for which Kendall wrote a number of political satires during 1879 and 1880 under the *nom de plume* of "A Mopoke" or "The Mopoke".

The *Punch* is the *Melbourne Punch*, which published several cartoons in 1880 representing the Roman Catholic vote as an Irishman's pig bearing the face of Sir John O'Shanassy, who figures as the hero of the satire under the name of "Sir Jack".

Sir John, Premier of Victoria three times between 1857 and 1863, was the political leader of the Irish Catholics, especially in opposing the secular system of education created by the Victorian Education Act of 1870 and in demanding a special grant for Catholic schools. Thus he tried to influence in turn the chief protagonists in Victorian politics at this period: Sir Graham Berry, leader of the Liberal Party, popular orator, radical, and protectionist, Premier from 1875 to 1880, and James Service, leader of the conservative party, a successful businessman, moderate conservative, and freetrader.

After five years in office Berry was defeated in the elections of February 1880, and Service became Premier. After he failed to carry his Reform Bill he secured a dissolution, but lost his majority in the elections of July 1880 and Berry again became Premier. Kendall's interpretation of the role played by "Sir Jack" in the July elections is confirmed in part by H. G. Turner's *History of the Colony of Victoria*, which states that, whilst Berry's oratory swung public opinion against Service, "Another adverse factor was a sectarian one. Sir John O'Shanassy, having failed to win Mr Service to his views on education matters, had declared war against him, and his influence alienated many votes."

Kendall's animus against Methodists, which is expressed with some bitterness in a number of his satires, probably derived from his resentment at the disapproval of his mother shown by members of the Kendall family who were strict Methodists.

Professor C. H. Pearson, a distinguished historian, entered Victorian politics in 1878, supported Berry as a commissioner on their constitutional reform mission to England, and afterwards served as Minister of Public Instruction.

Daniel Henderson, a supporter of Berry, was so dark-skinned that he was known as "Henderson Africanus", dubbed "the ebony politician", and cartooned in *Melbourne Punch* as an American negro or nigger minstrel—hence Kendall's "nig", i.e. "nigger".

Sir John Madden, a leader of the Victorian Bar, was Minister of Justice in the Service Ministry of 1880. In 1893 he became Chief Justice of Victoria.

And he tickled his friends by comparing the vote
Of the Catholic crowd to that gentleman big
With a snout and four trotters—the "Irishman's Pig".

And an equally "funny" old artist whose lunch
Is the meagre effect of his earnings from *Punch*
In a fishy back tavern fell in with the scribe,
Who slung him five bob by the way of a bribe;
And the fruit of this tip was a "picture" full "fig"
Of the Catholic vote as an "Irishman's Pig".

And the Mawworms who move in the Methodist sphere,
And are known by the size of the hoof and the ear,
Went hawking round *Punch* with the "pleasant" thing in,
And they laughed at the "joke", and they stuck to the "tin";
And Berry and Pearson, and Henderson—"nig"—
Roared out with delight at the "Irishman's Pig".

But a certain large party, whose name is Sir Jack,
Determined to pay them with interest back.
He bided his chance, and, a short while ago,
When the country was canvassed by Berry and Co.,
While the mob were "about" in the orthodox rig,
He quashed the whole crowd with the "Irishman's Pig"!

And Service the canny, of countenance bland,
Went crawling to Jack with the cap in his hand;
And said, "If you suffer my crew to go in,
I will fight for your party through thick and through thin."
"All right," answered Jack—"if you don't I will dig
Your grave, my bold boy, with the 'Irishman's Pig'."

So Service crept in, and the "shepherds" were sold,
And Berry and Company howled in the cold;
And Ministers giggled and collared the screw,
But kicked at their debt as most Ministers do.
Each *man* of them grew too immense for his rig,
And they laughed at the claims of the "Irishman's Pig".

The prospect looked rosy, and so did the pay;
And therefore they kicked the old ladder away.
"To pot with your Porker!" cried Service, in glee,

"He may grunt on for ever—he cannot hurt me!"
"Just wait, my fine fellow," said Johnny the big,
"And I'll give you a taste of the 'Irishman's Pig'."

Accordingly Jack, of that article rough,
Has given a "taste" that is more than enough;
For, pelted by censure, stale carrots, and eggs,
The tail of bold Service is under his legs.
And Madden is weeping and "wooling" his wig;
And the source of this woe is—the "Irishman's Pig".

The moral of this—it is not very long,
The whole can be put in one verse of a song;
What happened to Berry—to Service and Co.
May happen to others who think that they know
The road to success and a salary big
By kicking the ribs of the "Irishman's Pig".

And therefore we warn them to heed in good time
The fate of the parties embalmed in this rhyme.
A careful review of the Melbourne mistake
Would make our own Government wider awake.
It never would do for our Ministers big
To go to the wall through the—"Irishman's Pig".

A BOG-BOROUGH EDITOR

He may have been a barber's clerk,
    Or meek suburban draper,
But now the little pup can bark—
    He "runs" a country paper.

No doubt the "plant" for many years
    Was, like his garret, rented;
For ah, his coppers went in beers,
    And when he swiped he—*meant it*!

But, having dropped across a spouse,
    By dint of cheek and credit,
He popped into a larger house,
    And got his wife to edit.

He needn't beg for drinks at bars,
    For now the rag is floated;
And Mrs Jenkins writes the "pars",
    And Mr J. is—bloated.

By shouting now and then for rum,
    (God help his wretched readers!)
He gets a half-grown pothouse "bum"
    To "bullock" at his leaders.

My hero's paunch is full and fat;
    But it is darkly hinted
He nearly starves the Vernon rat
    By whom his trash is printed.

He doesn't slight his brace of friends,
    The paste-pot and the scissors,
Because through them he gains his ends,
    And, eke, his morning "fizzers".

His strong, substantial better-half
    Earns all his pocket-money;
And if he lost his wife, the calf
    Would feel extremely "funny".

(If grammar, reader, you should miss
    In the preceding stanza,
Just let me rip, and look at this
    As mere extravaganza.)

My Jenkins is the lad of lads
    (Don't interrupt, you scorner)
To poke about for shilling "ads."
    In every hole and corner.

I do believe that he would munch
    The mud of half the Tiber,
To get outside a glass of punch,
    Or at a new subscriber.

You'll meet him by the musty tap
    In yonder dirty shanty;
And, oh! he's not the sort of chap
    To edit Kant or Dante!

He's better at the little game
    Of cracking up clodhoppers;
And so he carries out his aim,
    And so he collars coppers.

If bumpkins Billy gets a scar,
    You may depend upon it
'Twill form the subject of a "par"—
    The topic of a sonnet.

When Mrs Tompkins cuts the corn
    That on her toe has sprouted,
Our canny printer blows his horn
    And tells the world about it.

No advertising booby need
    Go far to get a "puff" up.
In juggling Jenk he'll find indeed
    The boy to pile the "bluff" up.

In fact, the "dishclout" every time
    Comes bristling out with *locals*
(The Lord forgive me for the rhyme)
    About pig-headed yokels.

You see, my friend is wide awake!
    His game—I'd like to try it,
Because I'm very sure I'd make
    A d——d good living by it.

He write a leader! Why to tell
    The honest truth, O neighbour,
His wife can't teach him how to spell—
    She's given up the labour.

She worked for years; but then it's clear
    His head is like a boulder.
The bullock sports a yard of ear
    Above each shaggy shoulder.

But yet, by jobbing "on the cheap",
    And cadging round and blowing,
He gathers in enough to keep
    His hurdy-gurdy going.

As doubtless reader you will guess,
    This pert potato skinner
Pops up to represent the "press"
    At every country dinner.

Just reckon him from toe to pate;
    His mouth you see is ample.
It strikes me of the Fourth Estate
    He forms a sorry sample.

I think I'll drop the paltry pup—
    A clown is not a comet!
Here, waiter, pass the liquor up—
    I feel inclined to vomit.

The booby, when he bolts his punch,
    Will take my words for praises;
But hang it! I must go to lunch,
    And he may go to—blazes.

AN IDOL OF NEW BARATARIA*

"He was naturally the idol of the young men of this country; and his defeat
therefore is a terrible blow to us all."

From a great Baratarian Weekly.

He was born—but in mercy I'll gallop along,
Nor bother the reader by making my song
    A big biographical poem:
Suffice it to mention he grew to a height
Which made him a very respectable sight—
    So much by the way of a proem.

In the days of his youth at a quarry he delved;
But the pick and the shovel in season were shelved
    For the sake of a tight little ferry.
He strove like a "nigger"—he worked "on the square",
And his manner was bland and his charges were fair,
    And his rowing was elegant very.

As manhood came on, he discovered a way
Of getting in front of his mates on the bay;
    And, being an orthodox liver
With plenty of "bottom", he quickly became
The equal of Shakespeare—Hurrah for the game
    Of making wood *fly* down the river!

---

* Edward Trickett, 1857-1916, famous sculler and winner of some 150
races, became a popular idol in Australia in 1876 when he won the first
"world championship" sculling title by defeating J. H. Sadler in England on
the Thames. He retained the title by defeating M. Rush in 1877 on the Par-
ramatta, and E. Laycock in 1879. Hence it was felt almost as a national
disaster when in 1880 Edward Hanlan took the world championship title
from Trickett by defeating him easily by four lengths in a challenge race on
the Thames. Hanlan repeated his victory in 1882, but in 1884 lost his
championship title to W. Beach. Hanlan was actually not a "son of the Yank"
as described here, but a Canadian, born in Toronto. The Australian press,
however, often called him an American.

Sir Joseph George Long Innes, 1834-96, a cultured lawyer, became a member
of the Legislative Assembly, Solicitor-General, Attorney-General, and finally
a judge of the New South Wales Supreme Court.

Larry Foley, 1851-1917, famous boxer, defeated opponents of all sizes, in-
cluding many heavyweights, although only a welterweight himself, and
became Australian champion in 1879. He afterwards trained many other
notable boxers and promoted boxing matches.

The equal of Shakespeare? Say rather that he
Who left us Othello is reckoned to be,
    In this era of rowing and cricket,
A very small thing in the eyes of the gent
For whom this delectable ballad is meant—
    The item, whose idol is Trickett.

(Allow me in brackets to playfully say
I'm sure that the fellow who worships today
    The fortunate sculler or batter
Would cut Mr Sophocles dead in the street,
And crawl to the first Larry Foley he'd meet—
    I'm confident as to the latter.

Such people you see in this country abound:
In the highest society many are found—
    Bear witness, my erudite Innes!
And the outcome is *this*, that while natives excel
At the scull and the bat and at boxing as well,
    They mentally rank amongst ninnies.)

But, let me return to the theme of my verse—
He prospered at rowing and so did his purse;
    And, afar and in every quarter,
His fame was established, because, you perceive,
He had a big arm under each flannel sleeve
    And could *shove* ahead wood through the water.

In this very peculiar colony, he
Who excels in propelling a piece of a tree
    Through a pond of some sort or the other
Is held to be one of the greatest on earth;
And the country he hails as the land of his birth
    Is proud to be reckoned his mother.

He hasn't a rival, excepting, no doubt,
The party who's handy at pitching about
    At sticks with a ball of dry leather.
And, as to the few who believe in the schools
Of sweetness and light, they are coupled with fools,
    And are out in the cold altogether.

My hero was petted, and feasted, and made
To forget his old life with the pick and the spade—
    His pockets with coin were distended!—
Alas, for the day when an oysterman "floored"
This idol of ours at propelling a board!
    Our name as a Nation is ended!

Bow down in the ashes! A son of the Yank—
A trader in shellfish, has driven a plank
    Ahead of the plank of our Trickett!
The country is steeped in the shadow at last—
Our national life is a thing of the past—
    We're beaten at sculling and cricket!

And this is the land where a Dalley was born!
Forgive me, my friend, if a flavour of scorn
    Is here with a colour of sorrow;
I'm often, you see, like a man that is ill
When I *know*, in our worship of animal skill,
    We'd starve a new Wentworth tomorrow.

Don't think for a moment I'm holding him low
Whose deeds with the scull have delighted us so!
    I've gloried to see him a winner.
I quarrel with those who would lift him on high
And crown him, and feast him, nor notice the sigh
    Of genius in want of a dinner.

This verse is the last that at present I'll trace—
Give animal pluck its legitimate place
    Among things that are worthy of note, man.
In *this*, the grave time of our national youth,
We need the strong writer and statesman, forsooth,
    As well as the excellent boatman.

THE GAGGING BILL*

"Is this your foe—this thing of froth and fume?
Whom came ye forth to combat—warriors, whom!"

HEBER adapted.

He, armed with a surpassing wit—
With humour, satire, scholarship,
Knew whom to spare, and whom to hit,
And hewed the latter "thigh and hip."

M.S.

---

* This satire was published in the *Freeman's Journal*, 7th June 1879. The "Gagging Bill" was the Parliamentary Powers and Privileges Bill which provided penal clauses to punish criticism of members of Parliament as breaches of Parliamentary privilege. Sponsored by the Parkes-Robinson Government in October 1878, it was passed by the Legislative Assembly of New South Wales but amended drastically by the Legislative Council, the Upper House playing the unusual role of defender of the people's liberties against the popular House. This led to a long and bitter conflict between the Assembly and the Council on constitutional powers and procedures, and the Bill was never passed. The New South Wales newspapers attacked the Bill as gagging the press and infringing freedom of speech.

Although Kendall wrote this satire hastily at the request of his editor, he stated in a letter: "My feelings were considerably excited over this gross attempt to gag the mouth of public opinion." His indignation led him to assault Henry Parkes, who had often befriended him warmly in the past. Afterwards he felt remorse and expressed his contrition publicly in his elegy the following year on Parkes' son Robert, excusing himself also by the plea:

I smote, in noon, the public foe,
But not the private friend.

Parkes was deeply hurt by the attack, but forgave Kendall later and secured for him his last position as Inspector of Forests.

Stephen Campbell Brown, M.L.A., lawyer and member for Newtown, 1864-81, a member of the New South Wales Council of Education, incurred Kendall's criticism by his support of secular public schools. He became Postmaster-General for 1881-2 and M.L.C. in the same years.

William Bede Dalley, brilliant lawyer, scholar, and orator, a friend and patron of Kendall, took a prominent part, as a member of the Legislative Council, in opposing the "Gagging Bill".

Draco, as archon of Athens, drew up a code of laws in 623 B.C. which became historic for their severity.

Tydides, a patronymic of Diomedes, son of Tydeus and one of the most eminent Grecian chiefs in the Trojan war.

Horatius Cocles single-handed held a bridge over the Tiber at Rome against the Etruscan army under Porsena, as celebrated in Macaulay's poem.

Not fair Urania's aid I now beseech;
Some sterner Muse should come to shape my speech—
Some nymph with less of heaven in her mould
Should fire my thoughts, and make my stanzas bold!
O Stephen Brown! thou dim nonentity—
I gladly dedicate this song to thee!
What though thy name is nothing and thy head
Is like a lighthouse when the light is dead—
What though thy leisured moments—hours of ease—
Are spent in reckoning costs and counting fees—
What though the sleek attorney in thy shout
Glares forth like "shady" linen hanging out,
Who knows but that with all thy froth and fudge,
Some ass in power may make thee yet a Judge!
Ah! in that day when thou hast leave to don
The wig, and put the awful ermine on—
If such a day should come—do not forget
Thy humble bard! by Jove, I'll fatten yet!

Now to the bitter theme a while delayed
By admiration for the Pitt-street blade:—
O ye, whose hearths and homes are in the land
Where Wentworth shone, and Lowe, and William Bland—
Where, in the lordly elder days, the fight
Was waged for Freedom's large and liberal light—
Where, side by side, such fathers fought as him
At whose pure name the patriot's eyes grow dim—
The noble Forbes, who risked his all to save
An infant nation from a shameful grave—
Where radiant Richard Windeyer struggled on
(The shining father of a shambling son)—
O ye, who live where all these elders drew
The sword, and toiled away their lives for you,
What drug hath passed your lips—what potion sealed
Your eyes, ye human cattle of the field?
Here in the land that rang with words august,
What subtle fiend has blinded you with dust?
Say have you by your conduct justified
The trust of old that looked to you with pride?
Can those whose grand grey heads are as a dream
Upon your present councils look and beam?
Ah, no indeed! From gleaming halls of Morn
Their glances fall: their high-exalted scorn.

Is yonder butcher with the faithless face
A proper man to sit in Thomson's place?
Is Hoskins, Murrumbidgee whaler, say,
A fit successor to the seat of Hay?
Where governed Arnold of the virile days,
What ass is this that sets its ears and brays?
Is feeble little William Windeyer fit
To grace the seat where Martin used to sit?
Are these the sort of men—and such as these—
To lift the State and shape the best decrees?
Are those that follow at their heels the band
To shed a living lustre on the land?

O hide for shame, ye foolish ones, and blind,
Who made a ruler of a bag of wind!
Who placed your freedom in the reach of sharks,
And fell from Pericles to—Henry Parkes!
Great statesman this! the upstart of a day
To dare to say what Bismarck would not say!
Pure patriot he who, with his motley crew,
Was fain to do what Draco would not do!
Fair leader this, who recently has tried
Across the neck of English rights to ride!
Is this your model ruler?—turn and shout,
Ye boobies, while I trot your idol out!
Here is the man who on an evil date
Was pitchforked hither through the devil's gate—
Who crouched for years outside the social pale
Nor showed his hoof, nor advertised his tail—
Whose cunning seized upon the earliest chance
When men were fooled by blatant utterance—
Who crept to power in his peculiar mode
And stuck at nothing on the nasty road—
Who ran with every wind, and gained his ends
By buying foes and sacrificing friends!
Is *this* your model ruler—yokels say?
Ah, hide your faces—turn and hide away!
Lo, here is he who tried to set his foot
On Freedom's flower and crush it leaf and root!
Who made a wild attempt to overreach
And kill that right august—our right of speech!
Who sought to quench the noble light that beams,
And shows him as he *is*—not as he *seems*!

A wretched flunkey in a "ducal" dress—
He bridle Liberty—*he* gag the Press!
He put it out—the fine imperial flame,
And make an English-speaking people tame!
A thing like him—a mushroom of the mire—
Is he the one to cope with lordly-fire?
You *know* he *is* not, and you also know
The littleness of him ye worshipped so!
The scales have fallen; and the day is nigh
When you will stamp him out—this living lie.
Then—then, the fathers who have turned in shame
Will look again and glory in your fame.
And in that radiant hour your act will crown
Your friends with fairer laurels than renown;
True friends who over you the aegis cast,
And fought the tyrant to the bitter last!
All hail, my Dalley, heated from the fight—
The shining champion of the cause of Right!
On thy victorious sword and bloodless crest,
The grateful eyes of three young nations rest.
Victoria waits with laurels past the sea;
And Queensland hath a radiant wreath for thee.
Thy own fair land has crowned thy brow with bays—
The garland of a higher prize than praise.
The love too deep and holy for acclaim
Shall shed a deathless lustre on thy name.
For when the tyrant in his evil hour,
Like black Tydides armed with fourfold power
Amazed our ancient friends and choked their speech,
Thou, strong and splendid, leaped into the breach,
And checked the wave, and waged so long the fight
Whose issue was thy glory night by night.
Like him who singly faced the foes of Rome
When Tiber's bridge was drowned in seething foam,
Thou hast the sovereign courage tried by fire—
The will that conquers, and the words of fire.
Nor, Muse, forget to hail the faithful few
Who round their chosen leader nobly drew—
Who helped with flaming lance and gleaming spear
To kill the hydra that was wallowing here!
On your illustrious heads a light divine,
Like God's own sunlight, shall from henceforth shine.

For this one fight whose trophies are your own
A people's blessings at your feet are thrown.
Be yours the honour—yours the civic wreath,
Who stamped a curse out—took away its teeth;
Who seized a social devil by the hand,
And saved from worse than death the startled land.
Your fame is own—that lordly flame which burns
Beyond the life of immemorial urns.

PAST AND FUTURE

THE LAST OF HIS TRIBE

He crouches, and buries his face on his knees,
    And hides in the dark of his hair;
For he cannot look up to the storm-smitten trees,
    Or think of the loneliness there:
        Of the loss and the loneliness there.

The wallaroos grope through the tufts of the grass,
    And turn to their covers for fear;
But he sits in the ashes and lets them pass
    Where the boomerangs sleep with the spear:
        With the nullah, the sling, and the spear.

Uloola, behold him! The thunder that breaks
    On the tops of the rocks with the rain,
And the wind which drives up with the salt of the lakes,
    Have made him a hunter again:
        A hunter and fisher again.

For his eyes have been full with a smouldering thought;
    But he dreams of the hunts of yore,
And of foes that he sought, and of fights that he fought
    With those who will battle no more:
        Who will go to the battle no more.

It is well that the water which tumbles and fills
    Goes moaning and moaning along;
For an echo rolls out from the sides of the hills,
    And he starts at a wonderful song:
        At the sounds of a wonderful song.

And he sees, through the rents of the scattering fogs,
    The corroboree warlike and grim,
And the lubra who sat by the fire on the logs,
    To watch, like a mourner, for him:
        Like a mother and mourner, for him.

Will he go in his sleep from these desolate lands,
    Like a chief, to the rest of his race,
With the honey-voiced woman who beckons, and stands.
    And gleams like a Dream in his face—
        Like a marvellous Dream in his face?

KOOROORA

The gums in the gully stand gloomy and stark;
A torrent beneath them is leaping;
And the wind goes about like a ghost in the dark,
Where a Chief of Wahibbi lies sleeping!
He dreams of a battle—of foes of the past,
But he hears not the whooping abroad on the blast,
Nor the fall of the feet that are travelling fast.
  Oh! why dost thou slumber, Kooroora?

They come o'er the hills in their terrible ire,
And speed by the woodlands and water;
They look down the hills at the flickering fire,
All eager and thirsty for slaughter.
Lo! the stormy moon glares like a torch from the vale,
And a voice in the beela grows wild in its wail,
As the cries of the Wanneroos swell with the gale—
  Oh! rouse thee, and meet them, Kooroora.

He starts from his sleep and he clutches his spear,
And the echoes roll backward in wonder,
For a shouting strikes into the hollow woods near,
Like the sounds of a gathering thunder.
He clambers the ridge with his face to the light,
The foes of Wahibbi come full in his sight—
The waters of Mooki will redden tonight.
  Go! and glory awaits thee, Kooroora.

Lo! yeelamans splinter, and boomerangs clash,
And a spear through the darkness is driven;
It whizzes along like a wandering flash
From the heart of a hurricane riven.
They turn to the mountains that gloomy-browed band,
The rain droppeth down with a moan to the land,
And the face of a chieftain lies buried in sand.
  Oh! the light that was quenched with Kooroora.

Tomorrow the Wanneroo dogs will rejoice,
And feast in this desolate valley;
But where are his brothers—the friends of his choice?

And why art thou absent, Ewalli?
Now Silence draws back to the forest again,
And the wind, like a wayfarer, sleeps on the plain,
But the cheeks of a warrior bleach in the rain.
    Oh! where are thy mourners, Kooroora?

SUTHERLAND'S GRAVE*

(The first white man buried in Australia)

All night long the sea out yonder—all night long the wailful sea,
Vext of winds and many thunders, seeketh rest unceasingly!
Seeketh rest in dens of tempest where, like one distraught with pain,
Shouts the wild-eyed sprite, Confusion: seeketh rest, and moans in
    vain!
Ah, but you should hear it calling, calling when the haggard sky
Takes the darks and damps of Winter with the mournful marshfowl's
    cry;
Even while the strong, swift torrents from the rainy ridges come
Leaping down and breaking backwards—million coloured shapes of
    foam!
Then, and then, the sea out yonder chiefly looketh for the boon
Portioned to the pleasant valleys, and the grave sweet summer moon:
Boon of Peace, the still, the saintly, spirit of the dewdells deep—
Yellow dells, and hollows haunted by the soft dim dreams of sleep.
All night long the flying water breaks upon the stubborn rocks—
Ooze-filled forelands burnt and blackened, smit and scarred with
    lightning shocks;
But above the tender sea-thrift—but beyond the flowering fern,
Runs a little pathway westward—pathway quaint with turn on turn—
Westward trending, thus it leads to shelving shores and slopes of mist:
Sleeping shores, and glassy bays of green and gold and amethyst!
There tread gently—*gently*, pilgrim; *there* with thoughtful eyes look
    round;
Cross thy breast and bless the silence: lo, the place is holy ground!
Holy ground for ever, stranger! All the quiet silver lights
Dropping from the starry heavens through the soft Australian
    nights—
Dropping on those lone grave-grasses—come serene, unbroken, clear,
Like the love of God the Father, falling, falling, year by year!
Yea, and like a Voice supernal, *there* the daily wind doth blow
In the leaves above the Sailor buried ninety years ago.

---

* Sutherland, a Scottish seaman on the *Endeavour*, died of consumption
several days after it anchored in Botany Bay. Captain Cook recorded in his
Journal on 1st May, 1770: "Last night Forby Sutherland, Seaman, departed this
Life and in the A.M. his body was buried ashore at the watering place, which
occasioned my calling the south point of this bay after his name."

BLUE MOUNTAIN PIONEERS

The dauntless three! for twenty days and nights
These heroes battled with the haughty heights;
For twenty spaces of the star and sun
These Romans kept their harness buckled on;
By gaping gorges, and by cliffs austere,
These fathers struggled in the great old year;
Their feet they set on strange hills scarred by fire,
Their strong arms forced a path through brake and briar;
They fought with Nature till they reached the throne
Where morning glittered on the great UNKNOWN!
There, in a time with praise and prayer supreme,
Paused Blaxland, Lawson, Wentworth, in a dream;
There, where the silver arrows of the day
Smote slope and spire, they halted on their way.
Behind them were the conquered hills—they faced
The vast green West, with glad, strange beauty graced;
And every tone of every cave and tree
Was as a voice of splendid prophecy.

THE BALLAD OF TANNA*

She knelt by the dead, in her passionate grief,
Beneath a weird forest of Tanna;
She kissed the stern brow of her father and chief,
And cursed the dark race of Alkanna.
With faces as wild as the clouds in the rain,
The sons of Kerrara came down to the plain,
And spoke to the mourner, and buried the slain.
　　Oh! the glory that died with Deloya.

"Wahina," they whispered, "Alkanna lies low,
And the ghost of thy sire hath been gladdened,
For the men of his people have fought with the foe
Till the rivers of Warra are reddened!"
She lifted her eyes to the glimmering hill,
Then spoke, with a voice like a musical rill,
"The time is too short; can I sojourn here still?"
　　Oh! the Youth that was sad for Deloya.

"Wahina, why linger," Annatanam said,
"When the tent of a chieftain is lonely?
There are others who grieve for the light that has fled,
But *one* who waits here for you only!"
"Go—leave me!" she cried. "I would fain be alone;
I must stay where the trees and the wild waters moan;
For my heart is as cold as a wave-beaten stone."
　　Oh! the beauty that mourned for Deloya.

"Wahina, why weep o'er a handful of dust,
When the souls of the brave are approaching?
Oh! look to the fires that are lit for the just,
And the mighty who sleep in Arrochin!"

---

* Tanna, one of the larger islands of the New Hebrides, was visited by
Kendall on his youthful whaling voyage in the South Pacific. Years later he
claimed in a descriptive article that the poem was inspired by an actual battle
between "the rival factions of Deloya and Alkanna" among the Tannese during
his visit.

Wahina—maiden.
Arrochin—Heaven.

But she turned from the glare of the flame-smitten sea,
And a cry, like a whirlwind, came over the lea—
"Away to the mountains, and leave her with me!"
    Oh! the heart that was broke for Deloya.

ON A SPANISH CATHEDRAL

Deep under the spires of a hill by the feet of the thunder-cloud trod,
I pause in a luminous, still, magnificent temple of God!
At the steps of the altar august—a vision of angels in stone—
I kneel, with my head to the dust, on the floors by the seraphim
     known.
No father in Jesus is near with the high, the compassionate, face;
But the glory of Godhead is here—its presence transfigures the place!
Behold, in this beautiful fane with the lights of blue heaven im-
     pearled,
I think of the Elders of Spain, in the deserts—the wilds of the world!

I think of the wanderers poor who knelt on the flints and the sands
When the mighty and merciless Moor was lord of the Lady of Lands.
Where the African scimitar flamed with a swift bitter death in its
     kiss,
The fathers unknown and unnamed found God in cathedrals like
     this!
The glow of His Spirit—the beam of His blessing—made lords of the
     men
Whose food was the herb of the stream, whose roof was the dome of
     the den.
And, far in the hills by the sea, these awful hierophants prayed
For Rome and its temples to be—in a temple by Deity made.

Who knows of their faith—of its power? Perhaps, with the light in
     their eyes,
They saw, in some wonderful hour, the marvel of centuries rise!
Perhaps in some moment supreme, when the mountains were holy
     and still,
They dreamed the magnificent dream that came to the monks of
     Seville!
Surrounded by pillars and spires whose summits shone out in the
     glare
Of the high—the omnipotent fires, who knows what was seen by
     them there?
Be sure, if they saw in the noon of their faith some ineffable fane,
They looked on the Church like a moon dropped down by the Lord
     into Spain.

And the Elders who shone in the time when Christ over Christen-
dom beamed
May have dreamed at their altars sublime the dream that their
fathers had dreamed.
By the glory of Italy moved—the majesty shining in Rome—
They turned to the land that they loved, and prayed for a Church
in their home.
And a soul of unspeakable fire descended on them; and they fought,
And laboured, a life for the spire and tower and dome of their
thought!
These grew under blessing and praise, as morning in summertime
grows—
As Troy in the dawn of the days to the music of Delphicus rose.

In a land of bewildering light where the feet of the season are
Spring's,
They worked in the day and the night, surrounded by beautiful
things.
The wonderful blossoms in stone—the flower and leaf of the Moor
On column and cupola shone, and gleamed on the glimmering floor.
In a splendour of colour and form, from the marvellous African's
hands
Yet vivid and shining and warm, they planted the Flower of Lands
Inspired by the patience supreme of the mute, the magnificent, Past,
They toiled till the Dome of their Dream in the firmament blossomed
at last!

Just think of these men—of their time—of the days of their deed,
and the scene!
How touching their zeal—how sublime their suppression of self
must have been!
In a city yet hacked by the sword, and scarred by the flame of the
Moor,
They started the work of their Lord, sad, silent, and solemnly poor.
These Fathers, how little they thought of themselves, and how much
of the days
When the children of men would be brought to pray in their Temple
and praise!
Ah! full of the radiant, still, heroic old life that has flown,
The merciful monks of Seville toiled on, and died bare and un-
known.

The music, the colour, the gleam, of their mighty Cathedral will be
Hereafter a luminous dream of the Heaven I never may see.
To a spirit that suffers and seeks for the calm of a competent creed,
This Temple whose majesty speaks becomes a religion indeed.
The passionate lights, the intense—the ineffable beauty of sound
Go straight to the heart through the sense, as a song would of sera-
    phim crowned.
And lo! by these altars august, the life that is highest we live,
And are filled with the infinite trust and the peace that the world
    cannot give.

They have passed—have the Elders of Time: they have gone; but
    the work of their hands,
Pre-eminent, peerless, sublime, like a type of Eternity stands!
They are mute, are the Fathers who made this Church in the century
    dim;
But the dome with their beauty arrayed remains, a perpetual hymn.
Their names are unknown; but, so long as the humble in spirit and
    pure
Are worshipped in speech and in song, our love for these monks will
    endure.
And the lesson by sacrifice taught will live in the light of the years
With a reverence not to be bought, and a tenderness deeper than
    tears.

A REWARD

Because a steadfast flame of clear intent
    Gave force and beauty to full-actioned life;
Because his way was one of firm ascent,
      Whose stepping-stones were hewn of change and strife;
      Because as husband loveth noble wife,
He loved fair Truth; because the thing he meant
To do, that thing he did, nor paused, nor bent,
    In face of poor and pale conclusions; yea,
Because of this, how fares the Leader dead?
    What kind of mourners weep for him today?
What golden shroud is at his funeral spread?
    Upon his brow what leaves of laurel, say?
    About his breast is tied a sackcloth grey,
And knots of thorns deface his lordly head.

THE FAR FUTURE

Australia, advancing with rapid winged stride,
Shall plant among nations her banners in pride,
The yoke of dependence aside she will cast,
And build on the ruins and wrecks of the Past.
Her flag on the tempest will wave to proclaim
'Mong kingdoms and empires her national name;
The Future shall see it, asleep or unfurl'd,
The shelter of Freedom and boast of the world.

Australia, advancing like day on the sky,
Has glimmer'd thro' darkness, will blazon on high,
A Gem in its glitter has yet to be seen,
When Progress has placed her where England has been;
When bursting those limits above she will soar,
Outstretching all rivals who've mounted before,
And, resting, will blaze with her glories unfurl'd,
The empire of empires and boast of the world.

Australia, advancing with Power, will entwine
With Honour and Justice a Mercy divine;
No Despot shall trample—no slave shall be bound—
Oppression must totter and fall to the ground.
The stain of all ages, tyrannical sway,
Will pass like a flash or a shadow away,
And shrink to nothing 'neath thunderbolts hurl'd
From the hand of the terror—the boast of the world.

Australia, advancing with rapid wing'd stride,
Shall plant among nations her banners in pride;
The yoke of dependence aside she will cast,
And build on the ruins and wrecks of the Past.
Her flag in the tempest will wave to proclaim,
'Mong kingdoms and empires her national name,
And Ages shall see it, asleep or unfurl'd
The shelter of Freedom and boast of the world.

I hope the above will not be considered disloyal. It is but reasonable to
imagine that Australia will in the far future become an independent nation—
that imagination springing as it does from a native-born Australian brain.—H.K.

THE SYDNEY INTERNATIONAL
EXHIBITION

(A Prize Poem published with the kind permission of
the Proprietors of the "Sydney Morning Herald")

Now while Orion, flaming south, doth set
A shining foot on hills of wind and wet—
Far haughty hills beyond the fountains cold
And dells of glimmering greenness manifold—
While August sings the advent of the Spring,
And in the calm is heard September's wing,
The lordly voice of song I ask of thee,
High deathless radiance—crowned Calliope!
What though we never hear the great god's lays
Which made all music the Hellenic days—
What though the face of thy fair heaven beams
Still only on the crystal Grecian streams—
What though a sky of new strange beauty shines
Where no white Dryad sings within the pines,
Here is a land whose large imperial grace
Must tempt thee goddess in thine holy place!
Here are the dells of peace and plenilune,
The hills of morning and the slopes of noon;
Here are the waters dear to days of blue,
And dark-green hollows of the noontide dew;
Here lies the harp, by fragrant wood winds fanned,
That waits the coming of thy quickening hand!
And shall Australia, framed and set in sea
August with glory, wait in vain for thee?
Shall more than Tempe's beauty be unsung
Because its shine is strange—its colours young?
No! by the full live light which puts to shame
The far fair splendours of Thessalian flame—
By yonder forest psalm which sinks and swells
Like that of Phocis, grave with oracles—
By deep prophetic winds that come and go
Where whispering springs of pondering mountains flow—
By lute-like leaves and many-languaged caves,
Where sounds the strong hosanna of the waves,

This great new Majesty shall not remain
Unhonoured by the high immortal strain!
Soon, soon, the music of the southern lyre,
Shall start and blossom with a speech like fire!
Soon, soon, shall flower and flow in flame divine
Thy songs, Apollo, and Euterpe, thine!
Strong, shining sons of Delphicus shall rise
With all their Father's glory in their eyes;
And then shall beam on yonder slopes and springs
The light that swims upon the light of things.
And therefore, lingering in a land of lawn,
I, standing here, a singer of the Dawn,
With gaze upturned to where wan summits lie
Against the morning flowing up the sky—
Whose eyes in dreams of many colours see
A glittering vision of the years to be—
Do ask of thee, Calliope, one hour
Of life pre-eminent with perfect power,
That I may leave a song whose lonely rays
May shine hereafter from these songless days.

For now there breaks across the faint grey range
The rose-red dawning of a radiant change.
A soft sweet voice is in the valleys deep
Where darkness droops and sings itself to sleep.
The grave mute woods, that yet the silence hold
Of dim dead ages, gleam with hints of gold.
Yon eastern cape that meets the straitened wave—
A twofold tower above the whistling cave—
Whose strength in thunder shields the gentle lea,
And makes a white wrath of a league of sea,
Now wears the face of peace; and in the bay
The weak spent voice of Winter dies away.
In every dell, there is a whispering wing—
On every lawn, a glimmer of the Spring—
By every hill, are growths of tender green—
On every slope, a fair new life is seen;
And lo! beneath the morning's blossoming fires,
The shining City of a hundred spires!
In mists of gold, by countless havens furled,
And glad with all the flags of all the World!

These are the shores where, in a dream of fear,
Cathay saw darkness dwelling half the year![1]
These are the coasts that old fallacious tales
Chained down with ice and ringed with sleepless gales!
This is the land that, in the hour of awe,
From Indian peaks the rapt Venetian saw![2]
Here is the long grey line of strange sea-wall
That checked the prow of the audacious Gaul!
What time he steered towards the southern snow,
From zone to zone, four hundred years ago![3]
By yonder gulf, whose marching waters meet
The wine-dark currents from the isles of heat,
Strong sons of Europe, in a far dim year,
Faced ghastly foes and felt the alien spear!
There, in a later dawn, by shipless waves,
The tender grasses found forgotten graves.[4]
Far in the west, beyond those hills sublime
Dirk Hartog anchored in the olden time:
There, by a wild-faced bay, and in a cleft,
His shining name the fair-haired Northman left.[5]
And, on those broad imperial waters far,
Beneath the lordly occidental star,
Sailed Tasman down a great and glowing space
Whose softer lights were like his lady's face.
In dreams of her he roved from zone to zone,
And gave her lovely name to coasts unknown;
And saw in streaming sunset everywhere

---

[1] According to that eminent authority, Mr. R. H. Major, and others, the Great Southern Land is referred to in old Chinese records as a polar continent, subject to the long polar nights.

[2] Marco Polo mentions a large land called by the Malays Lochac. The northern coast was supposed to be in latitude 10° S. (*Vide* Bennett, and others.)

[3] Mr. R. H. Major has discovered a map of *Terra Australis* dated A.D. 1542, and bearing the name of Le Testu, a French pilot. Le Testu must have visited these coasts some years before the date of the chart.

[4] The sailors of the Duyfhen, a Dutch vessel which entered Carpentaria, in A.D. 1605, were attacked by the natives. In the fray, some of the whites were killed. No doubt, these unlucky adventurers were the first Europeans buried in Australia. (*Vide* Woods, and others.) (Kendall's *Duyfhen* was the *Duyfken*—Ed.)

[5] Dirk Hartog left a tin plate, bearing his name, in Shark's Bay, Western Australia. It was last seen in A.D. 1803.

The curious beauty of her golden hair.[1]
By flaming tracts of tropic afternoon,
Where in low heavens hangs a fourfold moon,
Here, on the tides of a resplendent year,
By capes of jasper, came the buccaneer.[2]
Then—then the wild men, flying from the beach,
First heard the clear bold sounds of English speech;
And then first fell across a Southern plain
The broad, strong shadows of a Saxon train.
Near yonder wall of stately cliff that braves
The arrogance of congregated waves,
The daring son of grey old Yorkshire stood
And dreamed in a majestic solitude,
What time a gentle April shed its showers,
Aflame with sunset, on the Bay of Flowers.[3]
The noble seaman who withheld the hand,
And spared the Hector of his native land—
The single savage yelling on the beach
The dark strange curses of barbaric speech!
Exalted sailor! whose benignant phrase
Shines full of beauty in these latter days;
Who met the naked tribes of fiery skies
With great divine compassion in his eyes;
Who died like Him of hoary Nazareth,
That death august—the radiant martyr's death;
Who in the last hour showed the Christian face
Whose crumbling beauty shamed the alien race.
In peace he sleeps where deep eternal calms
Lie round the land of heavy-fruited palms.
Lo! in that dell, behind a singing bar,
Where deep pure pools of glittering waters are,
Beyond a mossy yellow gleaming glade,
The last of Forby Sutherland was laid—
The blue-eyed Saxon from the hills of snow
Who fell asleep a hundred years ago.
In flowerful shades, where gold and green are rife,
Still rests the shell of his forgotten life.
Far, far away, beneath some northern sky—
The fathers of his humble household lie;

---

[1] Abel Tasman's love for Maria Van Dieman is well known. Tasmania, and many of the islands and points on the N.W. coasts of Australia were named after her.

[2] Dampier.   [3] Botany Bay.

But, by his lonely grave, are sapphire streams,
And gracious woodlands where the firefly gleams;
And ever comes across a silver lea
The hymn sublime of the eternal sea.

On that bold hill, against a broad blue stream,
Stood Arthur Phillip in a day of dream:
What time the mists of morning westward rolled,
And heaven flowered on a bay of gold!
Here, in the hour that shines and sounds afar,
Flamed first old England's banner like a star;
Here, in a time august with prayer and praise,
Was born the Nation of these splendid days;
And here, this land's majestic Yesterday
Of immemorial silence died away.

Where are the woods that, ninety summers back,
Stood hoar with ages by the water-track?
Where are the valleys of the flashing wing,
The dim green margins, and the glimmering spring?
Where now the warrior of the forest race,
His glaring war-paint, and his fearless face?
The banks of April, and the groves of bird,
The glades of silence, and the pools unstirred,
The gleaming savage, and the whistling spear,
Passed with the passing of a wild old year!
A single torrent singing by the wave,
A shadowy relic in a mountain cave,
A ghost of fire in immemorial hills,
The whittled tree by folded wayside rills,
The call of bird that hides in hollows far
Where feet of thunder, wings of winter are—
Of all that Past—these wrecks of wind and rain,
These touching memories—these alone remain!
What sun is this that beams and broadens west?
What wonder this, in deathless glory dressed?
What strange sweet harp of highest god took flame
And gave this Troy its life, its light, its name?
What awful lyre of marvellous power and range
Upraised this Ilion—wrought this dazzling change?
No shining singer of Hellenic dreams

Set yonder splendour by the morning streams!
No god, who glimmers in a doubtful sphere,
Shed glory there—created beauty here!
This is the City that our fathers framed—
These are the crescents by the elders named!
The human hands of strong heroic men
Broke down the mountain, filled the gaping glen,
Ran streets through swamp, built banks against the foam,
And bent the arch and raised the lordly dome!
Here are the towers that the Founders made!
Here are the temples where these Romans prayed!
Here stand the courts in which their leaders met:
Here are their homes, and here, their altars yet!
Here sleep the grand old men whose lives sublime
Of thought and action shine and sound through time!
Who worked in darkness—onward fought their ways
To bring about these large majestic days—
Who left their sons the hearts and high desires
Which built this City of the hundred spires!

A stately Morning rises on the wing,
The hills take colour, and the valleys sing.
A strong September flames beyond the lea—
A silver vision on a silver sea.
A new Age "cast in a diviner mould"
Comes crowned with lustre, zoned and shod with gold!
What Dream is this on lawny spaces set?
What Miracle of dome and minaret?
What great mute Majesty is this that takes
The first of morning ere the song bird wakes?
Lo, this was built, to honour gathering lands,
By Celtic, Saxon, Australasian hands!

These are the Halls where all the flags unfurled
Break into speech that welcomes all the world.
And lo, our friends are here from every zone—
From isles we dream of, and from tracts unknown!
Here are the fathers from the stately space
Where Ireland is, and England's sacred face!
Here are the Norsemen from their strong sea-wall,
The grave grand Teuton and the brilliant Gaul!
From green sweet groves the dark-eyed Lusians sail,

And proud Iberia leaves the grape-flushed vale.
Here are the lords whose starry banner shines
From fierce Magellan to the Arctic pines.
Here come the strangers from the gates of day—
From hills of sunrise, and from white Cathay.
The spicy islands send their swarthy sons,
The lofty North, its mailed and mighty ones.
Venetian keels are floating on our sea:
Our eyes are glad with radiant Italy!
Yea, North and South and glowing West and East,
Are gathering here to grace our splendid feast!
The chiefs from peaks august with Asian snow,
The elders born where regal roses grow,
Come hither, with the flower of that fair land
That blooms beyond the fiery tracts of sand
Where Syrian suns their angry lustres fling
Across blind channels of the bygone Spring.
And, on this great auspicious day, the flowers
Of Labour glorify majestic hours.
The singing angel from the starry sphere
Of dazzling Science shows his wonders here.
And Art, the dream-clad spirit, starts, and brings,
From Fairyland her strange sweet glittering things.
Here are the works man did what time his face
Was touched by God in some exalted place.
Here glows the splendour—here, the marvel wrought
When Heaven flashed upon the maker's thought!
Yea, here are all the miracles sublime—
The lights of Genius and the stars of Time!
And, being lifted by this noble noon,
Australia broadens like a tropic moon.
Her white pure lustre beams across the zones;
The Nations greet her from their awful thrones.
From hence, the morning beauty of her name
Will shine afar, like an exceeding flame.
Her place will be with mighty lords, whose sway
Controls the thunder and the marching day:
Her crown will shine besides the crowns of kings
Who shape the seasons, rule the course of things.
The fame of her across the years to be
Will spread like light on a surpassing sea;
And graced with glory, girt with power august,
Her life will last till all things turn to dust.

To Thee, the face of Song is lifted now—
O Lord, to whom the awful mountains bow;
Whose hands unseen the tenfold storms control;
Whose thunders shake the spheres from pole to pole;
Who from the highest heaven lookest down,
The sea Thy footstool and the sun Thy crown;
Around whose Throne the deathless planets sing
Hosannas to their high, eternal King—
To Thee, the soul of Prayer this morning turns,
With faith that glitters and with hope that burns!
And, in the moments of majestic calm
That fill the heart in pauses of the psalm,
She asks Thy blessing for this fair young land
That flowers within the hollow of Thine hand!
She seeks of Thee that boon, that gift sublime,
The Christian radiance, for this hope of Time!
And Thou wilt listen; and Thy face will bend
To smile upon us—Master, Father, Friend!
The Christ to whom pure pleading heart hath crept,
Was human once, and in the darkness wept;
The gracious Love that helped us long ago
Will on us like a summer sunrise flow;
And be a light to guide the Nation's feet
On holy paths—on sacred ways, and sweet.

HY-BRASIL

"Daughter," said the ancient father, pausing by the evening sea,
"Turn thy face towards the sunset—turn thy face and kneel with me!
Prayer and praise and holy fasting, lips of love and life of light,
These and these have made thee perfect—shining saint with seraph's
　　sight!
Look towards that flaming crescent—look beyond that glowing
　　space—
Tell me, sister of the angels, what is beaming in thy face?"
And the daughter who had fasted—who had spent her days in prayer
Till the glory of the Saviour touched her head and rested there,
Turned her eyes towards the sea-line—saw beyond the fiery crest,
Floating over waves of jasper, far Hy-Brasil in the West.

All the calmness and the colour—all the splendour and repose
Flowing where the sunset flowered like a silver-hearted rose!
There indeed was singing Eden, where the great gold river runs
Past the porch and gates of crystal ringed by strong and shining ones!
There indeed was God's own garden sailing down the sapphire sea—
Lawny dells and slopes of summer, dazzling stream and radiant tree!
Out against the hushed horizon—out beneath the reverent day,
Flamed the Wonder on the waters—flamed, and flashed, and passed
　　away.
And the maiden who had seen it felt a hand within her own,
And an angel that we know not led her to the Lands unknown.

Never since hath eye beheld it—never since hath mortal, dazed
By its strange unearthly splendour, on the floating Eden gazed!
Only once since Eve went weeping through a throng of glittering
　　wings
Hath the holy seen Hy-Brasil where the great gold river sings!
Only once by quiet waters—under still, resplendent skies,
Did the sister of the seraphs kneel in sight of Paradise!
She the pure, the perfect woman, sanctified by patient prayer,
Had the eyes of saints of Heaven—all their glory in her hair;
Therefore God the Father whispered to a radiant spirit near—
"Show Our daughter fair Hy-Brasil—show her this and lead her
　　here."

But beyond the halls of sunset—but within the wondrous west,
On the rose-red seas of evening, sails the Garden of the Blest.
Still the gates of glassy beauty—still the walls of glowing light
Shine on waves that no man knows of: out of sound and out of sight.
Yet the slopes and lawns of lustre—yet the dells of sparkling streams
Dip to tranquil shores of jasper where the watching angel beams.
But, behold, our eyes are human, and our way is paved with pain,
We can never find Hy-Brasil—never see its hills again!
Never look on bays of crystal—never bend the reverent knee
In the sight of Eden floating—floating on the sapphire sea!

BIBLIOGRAPHY

A. POETICAL WORKS OF HENRY KENDALL

Poems and Songs. Sydney, J. R. Clarke; London, Sampson Low, Son, & Marston. 1862.

At Long Bay: Euroclydon. Broadsheet. Sydney (?). No imprint and no date, c. 1865.

The Glen of the White Man's Grave. Sydney, Hanson & Bennett. No date, c. 1866. This poem included, with variations, in *Leaves from Australian Forests* and later collections under the title of "The Glen of Arrawatta", and published in a revised and expanded form in 1881 retitled "Orara".

The Bronze Trumpet: A Satirical Poem by *. Sydney. 1866. No imprint. Dedicated to "The Shams, Political, Clerical, and Critical, of Sydney, and (in particular) to the Puny Punsters of Punch." There is sufficient evidence to indicate that Kendall was the author of this anonymous satire.

Leaves from Australian Forests. Melbourne, George Robertson. 1869. Some copies dated 1870.

Euterpe: An Ode to Music. Printed in the programme of the Festival to celebrate the opening of the New Town Hall, Melbourne, on 9th August, 1870. Music of the cantata by C. E. Horsley.

In Memoriam: Nicol Drysdale Stenhouse. Sydney. No imprint. No date, c. 1876.

Cantata. Written Expressly for the Opening Ceremony of the Sydney International Exhibition. Words by Henry Kendall, Esq., Music by P. Giorza. Sydney. Published by the Composer, 1879.

Songs from the Mountains. Sydney, W. Maddock; London, Sampson Low, Marston, Searle, and Rivington. 1880. The original edition contained "The Song of Ninian Melville" on pages 144-52. This political satire was considered libellous by the publisher, who suppressed the edition. Kendall replaced the satire with "Christmas Creek", and the book was issued early in 1881.

Orara. Melbourne, Art-Union of Victoria. 1881. Illustrated with 13 lithographed engravings after J. W. Curtis, Henry Reilly, John Cully, and other artists.

The Song of Ninian Melville. Sydney. No imprint. 1885. Edited by J. Whitley. This booklet also includes "A Tour of Hell", by "Frank the Poet" (Frank Goddard). Another edition was published at Parramatta, *Times* Printing Works. No date, c. 1903.

Poems of Henry Kendall. Prefatory Note by Philip J. Holdsworth. Edited (anonymously) by Alexander Sutherland. Melbourne, George Robertson & Co. 1886. First collected edition, containing 100 poems.

Poems of Henry Clarence Kendall. Edited, with memoir, by Alexander Sutherland. Melbourne, George Robertson & Co. 1890. The addition of the Christian name "Clarence" was based on the fact that Kendall adopted it for a brief period at the time of his marriage. This collection contains 96 poems.

Poems of Henry Clarence Kendall. With Memoir by Frederick C. Kendall. Revised and enlarged edition. Melbourne, George Robertson & Co. 1903. Contains 114 poems.

Poems. Miniature edition. Melbourne, Thomas C. Lothian. 1910.

The Poems of Henry Kendall. Edited, with a Biographical Note, by Bertram Stevens. Sydney, Angus & Robertson. 1920. Contains 224 poems. Portrait.

Selected Poems of Henry Kendall. Chosen by his son, Frederick C. Kendall, with preface and memoir. Sydney, Angus & Robertson. 1923. Contains 65 poems. Portrait.

Rose Lorraine and Other Poems. Illustrations by Rhys Williams. Sydney, W. H. Honey Publishing Co. No date; 1945?

NOTE. A definitive edition of Kendall's poems, including many poems not represented in previous collections, is now being prepared by Dr T. T. Reed.

B. SELECT LIST OF BIOGRAPHICAL AND CRITICAL REFERENCES

I. Books of General Reference

Barton, G. B., *Literature in New South Wales.* Sydney. 1866.

Barton, G. B., *Poets and Prose Writers of New South Wales.* Sydney. 1866.

Cambridge History of English Literature. Cambridge. 1916. (*Vide* Vol. 14, article on "Literature in Australia".)

Chambers's Cyclopaedia of English Literature. London. 1925. (*Vide* Vol. III, article on "Australasian Literature".)

Coombes, A. J., *Some Australian Poets.* Sydney. 1938. (*Vide* chapter on Kendall.)

Cross, Zora, *Introduction to the Study of Australian Literature.* Sydney. 1922.

Ewers, John K., *Creative Writing in Australia.* Melbourne. 1945.

Grattan, C. Hartley, *Australian Literature.* Washington. 1929.

Grattan, C. Hartley (Ed.), *Introducing Australia.* New York. 1942.

Grattan, C. Hartley, *Australia.* Berkeley. 1947. (*Vide* article on "Literature" by H. M. Green.)

Green, H. M., *Outline of Australian Literature.* Sydney. 1930.

Green, H. M., *Fourteen Minutes.* Sydney. 1944. (*Vide* section on Kendall.)

Green, H. M., *Australian Literature, 1901-1951.* Melbourne. 1951.

Hancock, W. K., *Australia.* London. 1930.

Ingamells, Rex, *Handbook of Australian Literature.* Melbourne. 1949.

Jose, A. W., and Carter, H. J. (Ed.), *The Australian Encyclopedia.* Sydney. 1925. (*Vide* article on "Literature" by A. T. Strong.)

Mennell, Phillip, *The Dictionary of Australian Biography.* London. 1892.

Miller, E. Morris, *Australian Literature.* Melbourne. 1940. (Bibliography).

Miller, E. Morris, and Frederick T. Macartney (Editor), *Australian Literature.* Sydney. 1955. (Bibliography).

Palmer, Nettie, *Modern Australian Literature*. Melbourne. 1925.

Serle, Percival, *A Bibliography of Australasian Poetry and Verse*. Melbourne. 1925.

Serle, Percival, *Dictionary of Australian Biography*. Sydney. 1949.

Stephensen, P. R., *The Foundations of Culture in Australia*. Sydney. 1936.

Turner, Henry Giles, and Sutherland, Alexander, *The Development of Australian Literature*. Melbourne. 1898. (*Vide* biography of Kendall by Sutherland.)

Walker, William, *Australian Literature: A Lecture Delivered at the Windsor School of Arts*. Sydney. 1864.

II. Books of Special Reference

Campbell, Roy, *Broken Record*. London. 1934. (Autobiography in which the South African poet discusses the influence exerted on him by Kendall.)

Coombes, A. J., *Notes on Selected Poems of Henry Kendall*. Sydney. 1928.

Hamilton-Grey, A. M., *Facts and Fancies about our Son of the Woods: Henry Clarence Kendall and His Poetry, etc.* Sydney. 1920.

Hamilton-Grey, A. M., *The Poet Kendall: His Romantic History, etc.* Sydney. 1926.

Hamilton-Grey, A. M., *Kendall; Our God-Made Chief, A Singer of the Dawn, etc.* Sydney. 1929.

Holdsworth, Philip J., Memoir of Kendall in "A Prefatory Note" to *Poems of Henry Kendall*. Melbourne. 1886.

Kendall, Frederick C., "A Memoir of Henry Kendall", introduction to *Poems of Henry Clarence Kendall*. Melbourne. 1903.

Kendall, Frederick C., "Memoir", introduction to his *Selected Poems of Henry Kendall*. Sydney. 1923.

Kendall, Frederick C., *Henry Kendall, His Later Years: a Refutation of Mrs Hamilton-Grey's Book, "Kendall; Our God-Made Chief"*. Sydney. 1938.

Kevin, J. W., *Henry Kendall: An Essay*. Sydney. 1902.

McCrae, Hugh, *My Father and My Father's Friends*. Sydney. 1935.

Malone, J. J., *Kendall, the Australian Poet*. Melbourne. 1904.

Malone, J. J., *Talks About Poets and Poetry*. Melbourne. 1915.

Martin, A. Patchett, "Concerning Australian Poets," introductory article in *Australian Poets 1788-1888* (Ed. D. B. W. Sladen). London. 1888.

Palmer, Vance, *A. G. Stephens: His Life and Work*. Melbourne. 1941.

Sladen, Douglas B. W. (Ed.), *Australian Ballads and Rhymes*. London. 1888. (*Vide* appendix, "A Study of Henry Kendall as a "Bush Poet".)

Sladen, Douglas B. W. (Ed.), *A Century of Australian Song*. London. 1888. (*Vide* introduction and reprint of the review of Kendall's MS poems in the London *Athenaeum*, 27th September, 1862.)

Sladen, Douglas B. W. (Ed.), *Adam Lindsay Gordon*, the Westminster Abbey Memorial Volume. London. 1934. (*Vide* reprint of Kendall's *Australasian* review of Gordon's *Bush Ballads and Galloping Rhymes*.)

Stable J. J. (Ed.), *The High Road of Australian Verse*. London. 1929. (*Vide* introduction.)

Stephens, A. G., *Australian Writers. A Critical Review for the Use of Schools. I. Henry Kendall*. Sydney. 1928.

Stevens, Bertram, *The Poems of Henry Kendall*. Sydney. 1920. (*Vide* introductory "Biographical Note".)

Sutherland, Alexander, *Poems of Henry Clarence Kendall*. Melbourne. 1890. (*Vide* introductory memoir.)

III. References in Periodicals

Allen, L. H., "The Magic Word", in *Art in Australia*, May 1923.

Bayldon, A. A. D., "Australian Poetry—a Review", in the *Lone Hand*, May 1907.

Daley, Victor J., "Writers and Their Ways", in the *Bulletin*, 18th October 1902.

Dalley, William Bede, "Henry Kendall", in *Sydney University Review*, December 1882.

"Evelyn" (George Oakley), "National Poetry", in the *Australasian Monthly Magazine*, August 1867; "Mr Kendall's Poetry", in the *Australasian*, 16th January 1869; "Leaves from Australian Forests", review in the *Colonial Monthly Magazine*, October 1869.

Hamilton, E., "Australian Poets: Henry Clarence Kendall", in the *Sydney Quarterly Magazine*, 1889.

Holdsworth, Philip J., "Henry Kendall", in the *Sydney Athenaeum*, 5th February 1876.

Jose, A. W., "Literature in Australia", in *The Times Literary Supplement*, 1st October 1932.

Kendall, Henry, Review of Gordon's *Bush Ballads and Galloping Rhymes*, in the *Australasian*, 25th June 1870; "Men of Letters in New South Wales", in *Punch Staff Papers*, 1872.

McCrae, George Gordon, "Henry Kendall: A Biography", in the *Australian Woman's Magazine and Domestic Journal*, January and February 1883.

Miller, E. Morris and Mackaness, G., "Kendall and Lawson", in *Biblionews*, First Series 1947-8, No. 22.

Moir, J. K., Bibliographical details on *Leaves from Australian Forests* and *Songs from the Mountains*, in *Biblionews*, January 1949.

Murdoch, Walter, "The Literary Output", in the 150th Anniversary of Australia Number of *The Times*, London, 26th January 1938.

Myers, Francis, "The Other Kendall", in the *Bulletin*, 17th September 1903; "Gordon and Kendall", in the *Bulletin*, 5th November 1903.

Reed, T. Thornton, "Kendall and Rose Bennett", in *Biblionews*, Vol. 5, No. 10, 1952.

Roderick, Colin, "Memorial Remarks at the Grave of Henry Kendall", in *Biblionews*, Vol. 7, No. 12, 1954.

Ross, Lloyd, "Writers and Social Progress: Henry Kendall on Thatcher", in the *Australian Observer*, 23rd August 1947.

Rowland, P. F., "The Literature of the Australian Commonwealth", in the *Nineteenth Century and After*, April 1902.

Salier, C. W., "Harpur and Kendall: Footnotes to a Friendship", in *Southerly*, No. 2, 1948.

Smeaton, W. H. O., "A Quartette of Australian Singers", in the *Centennial Magazine*, July 1889; "A Gallery of Australian Singers", in the *Westminster Review*, 1895.

Stephens, A. G., "Australian Writers: No. 1. Henry.Kendall", in the *Bookfellow*, 15th December 1919; "Kendalliana"—I, II, III, and IV, in the *Bulletin*, 11th June, 18th June, 9th July, and 16th July 1930; "The Praise of Kendall", in the same, 30th July 1930.

Stone, Walter W., "A Kendall Suppression—*Ninian Melville*", in *Biblionews*, First Series, 1947-8, No. 17; "Kendall's *Song of Ninian Melville*", *Ibid.*, No. 18; "Henry Kendall and 'Rose Lorraine' ", *Ibid.*, Fourth Series, 1951, No. 4; "Henry Kendall and Roy Campbell", *Ibid.*, Vol. 7, 1954, No. 4; "The Rev. Dr T. Thornton Reed and his Kendall Collection", *Ibid.*, Vol. 7, 1954, No. 5.

Sutherland, Alexander, "Henry Clarence Kendall", in the *Melbourne Review*, Vol. VII, 1882.

Topp, S. S., "Australian Poets", in the *Melbourne Review*, April 1876.

Wilde, Oscar, "Australian Poets", in *Pall Mall Gazette*, 14th December 1888: review of *Australian Poets, 1788-1888*, edited by Douglas B. W. Sladen.

INDEX TO TITLES

INDEX TO FIRST LINES

INDEX TO SOURCES OF POEMS

A. COLLECTED POEMS

Beyond Kerguelen
Hy-brasil
Jim the Splitter
Mooni
Pytheas
Bill the Bullock Driver
Cooranbean
The Voice in the Wild Oak
Billy Vickers
Narrara Creek
Araluen
The Sydney International Exhibition
Christmas Creek
Orara
On a Spanish Cathedral
Galatea
Names Upon a Stone
Leichhardt
After Many Years
The Song of Ninian Melville (from copy of the suppressed
    edition in the Mitchell Library)

From *Poems of Henry Kendall* (ed. by A. Sutherland), 1886:

Blue Mountain Pioneers
Outre Mer

From *The Poems of Henry Kendall* (ed. by B. Stevens), 1920:

James Lionel Michael
Song of the Shingle-splitters
The Far Future

From Periodicals:

On a Street. *Town and Country Journal*, 12th April 1879.
The Austral Months. *Sydney Mail*, January to December
    1881.
Camped by the Creek. *Australian Journal*, November 1870.
The Late Mr A. L. Gordon: In Memoriam. *Australasian*, 2nd
    July 1870.
Sydney Harbour. *Punch Staff Papers*, 1872.

B. UNCOLLECTED POEMS

To Fanny. Copy supplied by Dr T. T. Reed.
In Memoriam: Archdeacon McEncroe. *Empire*, 27th August
    1868.
The Sawyer Who Works on the Top. *Freeman's Journal*, 30th
    August 1879.
The "Irishman's Pig". *Freeman's Journal*, 21st August 1880.
A Bog-borough Editor. *Freeman's Journal*, 15th May 1880.
An Idol of New Barataria. *Freeman's Journal*, 29th January
    1881.
The Gagging Bill. *Freeman's Journal*, 7th June 1879.
In Memoriam: Marcus Clarke, *Bulletin*, 3rd September 1881.